Praise for **Let Your Fears Make You Fierce**

"I celebrate Koya. She is not just a friend but an inspiration.
Koya's voice is needed in this world. She shares her stories of
transformation skillfully and gives us clear and easy-to-digest
mind and body recommendations to process fear and challenges to
live a healthier lifestyle. Koya's vulnerability and leadership shared
in this book will inspire readers worldwide to practice daily self-
care mentally, spiritually, and physically, and as a fellow vegan I
know she is taking
all the steps to make this world a better place."

— **Cory Booker**, United States Senator

"In *Let Your Fears Make You Fierce*, Koya shares stories and practical
recommendations cutting through the noise of our busy minds with
her realness and inspiring writing. She leads us towards embracing
flow and flexibility, helping us break the patterns of self-imposed
limitations to create more freedom in our lives."

— **Kimberly Snyder**, *New York Times* best-selling author of *The Beauty Detox*
book series and *Radical Beauty* and founder of Solluna

"Koya Webb is a living inspiration. Her presence in the world is
a blessing to countless individuals. From fitness to nutrition to
breaking negative paradigms, Koya lives what she teaches. This
book you're holding, *Let Your Fears Make You Fierce* is a jewel for
your transformation! Read it, practice the principles, and
your life will change for the better!"

— **Michael Bernard Beckwith**, founder and spiritual director,
Agape International Spiritual Center and best-selling
author of *Life Visioning*

"Koya Webb is a dynamic force whose black girl magic and magnetic energy is contagious. From yoga teacher to inspirational lifestyle coach, Koya has used her gifts to spread her glow power worldwide. She's a leader in the wellness space and a woman of color who is trailblazing a path for others to follow. In *Let Your Fears Make You Fierce*, Koya has created a map that takes readers on a journey of deeper self-discovery."

— **Latham Thomas**, women's wellness maven and best-selling author of *Own Your Glow*

"Koya has written an inspiring guide for anyone seeking to live a healthier life. Her stories of transformation offer clear and simple recommendations to process fear and challenges to wellness."

— **Dean Ornish, M.D.**, best-selling co-author of *UnDo It!*

"Koya has a beautiful way of transforming the lives of others with her work. In *Let Your Fears Make You Fierce* she shares very practical ways to live a healthy, balanced lifestyle while motivating the reader with her candid stories of triumph after tragedy. It's a great book for everyone looking to improve their lives."

— **Karyn Calabrese**, restauranteur, holistic health expert, and author of *Soak Your Nuts*

"This book will certainly help you gain clarity of purpose and live a more intentional life."

— **Light Watkins**, author of *Bliss More: How to Succeed in Meditation Without Really Trying*

"*Let Your Fears Make You Fierce* is a powerful book that guides you through an incredible journey to face your fears with love and compassion. Koya Webb's words are transparent, insightful, engaging, and encouraging, drawing upon the ancient wisdom traditions to support your growth. Reading this book made me take an honest look at my fears and instead of running away from them, I now embrace them and say yes, and that is when the transformation happens."

— **Airrion Copeland**, senior vice president of programs, Mercy For Animals

Let Your Fears Make You FIERCE

Hay House Titles of Related Interest

Let Your Fears Make You FIERCE

how to turn common obstacles into seeds for growth

KOYA WEBB

HAY HOUSE, INC.
Carlsbad, California • New York City
London • Sydney • New Delhi

Published in the United States by: Hay House, Inc.: www.hay house.com® • *Published in Australia by:* Hay House Australia Pty. Ltd.: www.hayhouse.com. au • *Published in the United Kingdom by:* Hay House UK, Ltd.: www.hayhouse. co.uk • *Published in India by:* Hay House Publishers India: www.hayhouse. co.in

Cover design: Kathleen Lynch • *Interior design:* Nick C. Welch
Interior photos: Robert Reiff Photography • *Interior illustrations:* Deun Ivory

Library of Congress Cataloging-in-Publication Data

Names: Webb, Koya, author.
Title: Let your fears make you fierce : how to turn common obstacles into seeds for growth / Koya Webb.
Description: Carlsbad, California : Hay House, [2019]
Identifiers: LCCN 2019000167 | ISBN 9781401956950 (tradepaper : alk. paper)
Subjects: LCSH: Fear. | Self-realization.
Classification: LCC BF575.F2 W4195 2019 | DDC 152.4/6--dc23 LC record available at https://lccn.loc.gov/2019000167

Tradepaper ISBN: 978-1-4019-5695-0
E-book ISBN: 978-1-4019-5696-7
Audiobook ISBN: 978-1-4019-5705-6

10 9 8 7 6 5 4 3 2 1
1st edition, June 2019

Printed in the United States of America

SUSTAINABLE FORESTRY INITIATIVE
Certified Chain of Custody
Promoting Sustainable Forestry
www.sfiprogram.org
SFI-01268
SFI label applies to the text stock

For those who want to heal their pain and trauma so they can step confidently into the greatest version of themselves

Contents

get loved up morning prayer

We are LOVE.

*We release all of the limiting beliefs that
block us from our greatness.*

We are open to the infinite possibilities of love in our lives.

*We are prepared to meet all assignments
with a loving heart and joyous spirit.*

*We are ready to heal any place within us
holding on to residual fear.*

*We pray for guidance in flowing with clear
intentions and pure thoughts.*

*We feel love, beauty, and divine intelligence
in every cell of our body.*

We radiate good vibes wherever we go.

*We are patient with ourselves and others as our
journey of truth reveals itself daily.*

*We embrace all experiences as opportunities to
grow and express gratitude.*

We know we are divinely supported and provided for.

We are grateful for our lives.

And so it is.

Ashé

Foreword

The moment Koya walked through the doors of Agape International, her presence was felt. She attended Sunday services, spiritual enrichment classes to further her knowledge base, and even speaking classes to enhance her powerful presentations.

Soon Koya began teaching vegan nutrition classes, holistic health classes, and doing demos at Agape. I even invited her to speak at our yearly Revelation Conference. When she stepped on stage she spoke as if she was waiting for the perfect opportunity to let her light shine.

And shine she did; her presence and radiance can be seen and felt wherever she goes, and it is my joy to watch her bring this new book to life. Reading the insights she shares about transformation, you will discover that while the process isn't always easy, the rewards are priceless.

Her passion for encouraging a more holistic lifestyle from the inside out will inspire you to make more mindful choices in every area, from who you surround yourself with, to what you listen to, and just as importantly, what you eat.

So much of what happens to us in life is meant to make us better and not bitter. It's easy to overlook that when it seems the entire universe is conspiring against you; however, what you will discover in immersing yourself in this beautifully written book is how to move past the pain into a place of promise for a life that is purposeful and powerful.

Koya is a natural leader, visionary, and gifted teacher. I look forward to continuing to watch her unfold into bolder versions of herself—and bringing along others so that they can do the same. She's the real deal!

When you read this book, do so with the intention of making small shifts that will lead to bigger blessings. You won't conquer all the fears at once—no one does—but consistency is the key to lasting change, and if you get it down on the inside that you are worthy of doing the work, you will be a fierce force to be reckoned with, and that's just what the world needs you to be.

— Michael Bernard Beckwith,
Founder, Agape International Spiritual Center and author of
Life Visioning

Introduction

you are more than your fears

There are two ways to live: in a state of love or in a state of fear.

In a state of love, you are confident, joyful, and inspired. You hear the desires of your heart and soul and live in accordance with them. You radiate the vibration of love and attract positive energy, abundance, and everything in alignment with that vibration of love. In that state of love, you are your best and highest self. You are fierce.

In a state of fear, you live in doubt, insecurity, and scarcity. Fear drowns out the voices of your heart and soul, so you can't live in alignment with their guidance. Fear holds you back from living your truth and achieving your full potential. Fear blocks your blessings and keeps you from experiencing the fullness of life. Fear prevents you from overcoming obstacles successfully. Over time, unresolved fear leads to sadness, confusion, and disease.

Clearly, living in love is where we want to be! In love, everything is possible. I'm happy, hopeful, and upbeat. There isn't a goal I can't reach, a dream I can't realize, or a challenge I can't overcome. I make good decisions, and my business thrives. My relationships become deeper and more meaningful. New, supportive people enter my life. I make time for self-care, and I thrive physically, emotionally, and spiritually. Everything is in alignment, and I am in a beautiful flow with the people and energy around me.

It's easy to spot others who are in the state of love. Filled with passion and purpose, they seem to glow from within. They take risks and thrive on the uncertainty. They stand in their power, confident in who they are, what they want their life to be, and how they are going to get there.

It's also pretty easy to spot the folks who are living in fear. They're *stuck*. Stuck in their current situation—an unhappy one—afraid to take the next step, afraid to take a risk, afraid of what others might think, afraid of doing or saying the wrong thing. Maybe you have a friend who always talks about starting a new business but never does anything to get it off the ground. Or a sister who is in an unhealthy relationship, and knows it, but won't make a move to leave. Or a co-worker who has given up on trying to eat a healthy diet and get more fit because she hasn't been able to make these habits stick in the past. But fear isn't just *I'm afraid of* [fill in the blank]. The root of all negative emotions is fear. If you have a loved one who is filled with anger, resentment, jealousy, worry, shame, or envy, they're living in fear too.

Or maybe this sounds a lot like you. It certainly sounds like me sometimes. Even though I coach others on how to live in love and have created an entire community dedicated to holistic health and healing, I'm not perfect. Sometimes life throws me a curveball and I can't find the love right away. Fear takes over and I start to doubt myself. What if people don't like my new video series? Will my new client think I'm good enough to help her? Who am I to think I have enough experience or knowledge to mentor others? I get doubtful and frustrated and close myself off from new opportunities.

The fact is we usually don't live in just one state or the other. We often toggle back and forth between the two. One day you may feel like superwoman, and the next day you're too timid to speak up in a meeting.

But here's the thing: We don't have to stay in a state of fear at all. It's not inevitable. It's not just how life is. It may be part of the human experience, but it's not a part of the human condition. Whether consciously or not, we choose to live in a state of fear by allowing our fears to have power over us. The good news is we can choose love instead. We can choose to learn from our fears and use them to help us grow and thrive. We can choose to turn them from an obstacle into a launching pad. We can choose to allow them to get us closer to our authentic selves and obtain our most ideal reality. We can choose to use our fears to make us stronger. And when we do that, we become what I call *fierce*.

Being fierce isn't about avoiding fear or never feeling fear again. That's impossible. Being fierce is about knowing how to handle fear and being able to move out of the state of fear and back into the state of love. We can't eliminate fear—or obstacles, challenges, and difficulties—but we can make them opportunities for growth.

FACING FEAR

I know a lot about fear because I've lived in it. I know firsthand how abuse, depression, and suffering can make you afraid to live and crush your dreams. I know fear isn't easily dismissed. It can be deeply rooted, so embedded that it seems like it's a part of *who you are*. It can be overwhelming, especially if you've experienced trauma. I've known fear since I was a child: the stomach-clenching fear of being called on in class, the crushing fear of disappointing my parents, and the soul-numbing fear after a sexual assault. It wasn't until after a devastating track and field injury that I realized the healing powers we all possess.

I have yoga to thank for helping me turn the corner on my healing. It may sound trite and easy, but it's true—and it was very, very hard. Over several long, difficult months of pain and doubt, a regular yoga practice helped me find strength and flexibility in my body, gain confidence and emotional resilience, and reconnect with my spiritual side. Yoga became my best friend, and I now had hope.

That's when I realized that we all need to support the total self—body, mind, and spirit—to release fear. It isn't enough to be physically fit if the spirit is thirsty for attention. Or to be in a good mental state if the body is weak and tired. Only when all three aspects of the self are in balance and we take the time to attend to each of them through self-care practices such as good nutrition, yoga, and meditation does fear lose its grip and we thrive. We thrive because without fear, we can hear the authentic self and live in alignment with its guidance.

Your authentic self is *who you are*. It's your heart and soul. It's what is true for you and who you want to be. Your authentic self should guide your life, but fear can block your ability to hear it. Release your fears, and you can connect with your authentic self in a genuine and meaningful way to discover your deepest truths and desires. You'll know who you want to be, the life you want to lead, and the people with whom you want to surround yourself. You'll soon be empowered to make choices that support those goals.

That's my ultimate hope for you: that, living according to your soul's guidance and confidently moving forward in alignment with everything you believe, you can achieve your dreams. It all starts with taking care of those fears and strengthening yourself physically, mentally, and spiritually.

Helping as many people as possible is my passion, one that has shaped my personal and professional path. I've grown from a certified personal trainer and life coach to a certified yoga instructor, meditation teacher, and graduate of the Institute for Integrative Nutrition so that I can bring total wellness to my clients and my community. From chakra balancing to plant-based eating and affirmations, visualization, self-reflection, and gratitude, my holistic healing approach embraces healing practices that support the whole self and foster alignment between heart and soul. These practices have changed my life, and I've watched as, used in unison, they've changed the lives of countless others. Those who work with me privately, participate in my personal online community, or are part of my Get Loved Up community, dedicated to spreading love through yoga, plant-based eating, and eco-friendly living, have all experienced their benefits.

Through my workshops, courses, podcasts, yoga retreats, and yoga teacher training courses, I've helped thousands of people deal with all sorts of issues: the stress of starting a new business, the lack of motivation to achieve a fitness goal, the disapproval from friends and family regarding significant life-style changes, the sadness over the end of a relationship, the worry at not being good enough to succeed. From the young women struggling with being on their own to the new entrepreneurs worrying about the success of their next venture to the celebrities seeking longevity, all my clients struggle with fear. It's at the heart of each and every issue, and I know addressing the fear is the first thing we have to do together. If you don't, you'll never solve your current problem, and more importantly, you'll keep struggling, preventing you from becoming your very best self.

Identifying and overcoming our individual fears is essential for our personal health and well-being, but it's also critical for the health and well-being of our entire world community and planet. Fear breeds fear. The more people living in fear, the more fear in the world, and the more anger, insecurity, abuse, pain, greed, selfishness, corruption, and violence right along with it. That's not the world I want to live in, and I know you don't either. The answer is to confront our fears using every self-care practice in our basket and bring more love into the world.

How This Book Is Organized

In *Let Your Fears Make You Fierce*, I'll walk you step by step through the process of moving from fear-based living to love-based living.

In *Part I: What Are You Scared Of?*, I'll help you to identify your fears and give you the tools you need to transform them.

First, we'll look at the four most common types of fear and shift your mind-set on them, opening you up to viewing fear as an opportunity rather than a roadblock. Think of fear as physical pain, an indication that something needs your attention. It's not good; it's not bad—it just is. We can use the fear to understand and address the underlying cause of the pain—the real issue holding you back from living in love. It sounds so simple, but this shift is incredibly transformational. You've already loosened fear's hold on you by choosing to read this book.

Part II: Live Your Truth is all about reconnecting with your heart and soul by balancing your chakras and opening yourself up to new experiences, one of the best ways to deepen your self-knowledge. Once you identify what you truly want out of life, you'll use affirmations, visualization, and discipline (yes, discipline!) to help you achieve it. You can then unapologetically follow the callings of your soul and move fiercely into your future doing what you love. Using clarity and focus, you will concentrate your energy to accomplish what matters most to you now and avoid the distractions that can sabotage your efforts.

Each chapter in the book contains daily self-care and healing practices to help you choose love over fear every day. Since fear is such a common emotion, practicing self-care and self-love on a daily basis is as necessary as taking a shower. You'll find the three most important ingredients to your "spiritual shower"—affirmations, yoga, and meditation—in every chapter. We'll use them to wash off fear and lather up with love.

To put you in the best possible mind-set to absorb the material you will be reading, an affirmation opens each chapter. Affirmations are positive statements to inspire and motivate. Saying them twice daily, first thing in the morning and before bed at night, gets your brain working on making them come true. It's a fantastic way to begin and end your day on a powerful note. If you're new to affirmations, try writing them down too. The affirmations in each chapter will put out good energy into the universe and bring more positive energy and love your way.

Yoga is more than poses or a workout. It's a mindfulness practice to help balance your mind, body, and spirit. It's a practice that inspires growth and transformation, no matter how long you've been on the mat. Yoga taught me to honor my body's limits, move more mindfully, and create space for stillness. And when life doesn't make sense, yoga helps me cope. Trust me: yoga can better your life.

If you've never tried yoga before, that's okay. I've designed the practices in this book to meet you where you are. Open your heart to yoga's possibilities, take it slow, and listen to your body as you follow my directions. Feel free to do the pose in each chapter in your street clothes. Just get on the floor and relax. If you'd like to start a full yoga practice now, try Sun Salutations A and B as a warm-up and the Get Loved Up Yoga Flow, both available on my website, koyawebb.com. For those of you who regularly practice yoga, I invite you to approach the poses in the book with a heightened mindfulness and deepen your practice. Wherever you are on your yoga journey, come as you are to honor and love yourself. Yoga will help you grow stronger, get centered, and spark your creativity each and every day.

Meditation is when I listen to my heart and soul and connect with Spirit. Spirit guides my path and will guide yours if you let it. It's so difficult to figure out what your authentic truth is. There is so much external noise crowding out your inner voice, from media to your loved ones, boss, teachers, and neighbors. Through meditation and deep breathing, I silence that noise, quiet my mind, and tap in to my inner guide. Connecting with that inner guide is so important. If you don't know who you are, how can you know where to go?

The meditations in the book will help you to go within to work things out and become more aware of who you are. In meditation, we focus on the breath because your breath is always present. Paying attention to your breath will help anchor you in the present moment and silence the thoughts, emotions, and sounds that can overwhelm you and prevent you from hearing your inner guide. If you haven't meditated before, I encourage you to give it a try and be patient with yourself. Meditation is called a practice because, well, it requires practice!

Yoga and meditation have brought a new level of mindfulness into my life. They've been the most beautiful gifts I've ever received, and I love sharing them.

The other prompts and practices included throughout the book will also help you heal from pain, build your confidence, strengthen your mind, and de-stress your body. I encourage you to try each practice, but it's most important that you find the practices that work for you. We each have our own way. Try them all and include the ones that feel best to you in your daily wellness routine.

LET'S BE FIERCE

Everyone experiences challenges in life, from minor setbacks to major disappointments. Perhaps you've experienced a terrible performance review, the failure of a new business, the end of a relationship, a health crisis, or the death of a loved one. Maybe you're feeling stuck or lost or uncertain about the future. At times like these, it's natural to feel fear.

The question is, do you let your challenges and fears conquer and control you, or do you look fear in the face and say, "I've got enough love for you"? Confronting fear with love transforms those fears into opportunities to grow and heal.

It's okay to feel fear. We all feel fear at one time or another. What matters is what you do with that fear. Do you let it stop you, or do you turn it into positive energy that launches you forward?

I don't want fear to stop you from achieving your dreams. I want to help you let go of the power fear has over you and connect you with the strength you have inside of you. You can choose to live in alignment with fear. But if you decide to live in alignment with love, you'll find a good friend in this book. Love is always there. All you need to do is choose.

PART I

What Are You Scared Of?

affirmation practice

Say this affirmation several times upon waking in the morning and before going to bed at night:

I am patient with myself and others as truth and love reveal themselves through me daily.

CHAPTER ONE

The Path of Fear

On the track, I felt invincible. From the moment I joined the track team in middle school, I knew I'd found my place. I loved everything about running: the strength and power of my body, the satisfaction of improving my times, the challenge of mastering the events of the heptathlon, the discipline of training for hours each day, the thrill of competition, and the camaraderie of my teammates. In high school, I ate, slept, walked, and talked track. I *was* track to the folks in my town of Humboldt, Tennessee. And I *loved* it. Track opened so many doors for me. Traveling to meets opened my eyes to different places and people and sparked a desire to see as much of the country and the world as possible. Track also helped me continue my education. With a full track scholarship, I was able to go to college and keep doing what I loved doing most for at least another four years. But even then my dreams were bigger: the Olympics. Competing against the world's best and being a positive role model for other young girls and athletes, especially of color, motivated me every day. My numbers were good enough that this wasn't a wild idea. With hard work and enough training, it could happen. *That is my future,* I thought.

My first year at Wichita State University went very well, and by sophomore year, I was slated to win the conference championship titles in two of my favorite events, the heptathlon and the high jump. One day when I was walking home from class, I felt a sharp, shooting pain in my lower back. All of a sudden, I was on the ground. I had no idea what was wrong. I hadn't fallen; I hadn't been injured. Just out of nowhere, wave after wave of pain pulsed through me. I was rushed to the doctor, and he said the words no athlete ever wants to hear: "I'm sorry. Your season is over. You have a stress fracture in your lower back."

What? I was in shock. *No way*, I thought, *I'm at the peak of my career. There's no way this is happening now.*

My coach was super nice and supportive and said I could still be on the team as a captain and help him . . . but I didn't want to hear about options like coaching. The only thing I wanted to hear was that I could get back on the track and compete again. I was heartbroken. I needed to make substantial gains for the Olympic trials if I had any chance of realizing that dream, and now, it seemed impossible.

Being sidelined was totally devastating, as though someone had dropped a 1000-pound safe on my head. I didn't know how to be without track and field. All of my time, effort, and energy had been focused on training, and suddenly I couldn't train anymore. My life was track and track was my life. My purpose was gone. My self-confidence plummeted. *What if I can never run track again? Now how can I make a difference in the world? What am I going to do with my life? What is my purpose?* I was in a very dark place, uncertain about the future and really, really sad. It was as if someone had died. And that someone was the me I knew as me.

After I broke down sobbing in her class one time too many, my teacher sent me to a counselor. While I don't remember her name or even what kind of counselor she was (the whole experience was a bit of a blur because I was such a mess, and I never saw her again), what I do remember—vividly—is that she suggested I try yoga. Yoga? Where did that come from? And who was she kidding? I was raised Southern Baptist in Humboldt, Tennessee. I didn't know much about this yoga thing, but I knew it wasn't going to be for me.

"Is it like worshipping Buddha?" I finally asked her.

"No," she assured me, "it's just stretching."

I wasn't too sure how stretching was going to heal a stress fracture or fix my life, but I'd pretty much just gotten kicked out of class, so I didn't feel that I had much of a choice.

My first yoga class was incredibly frustrating. I looked around the room and was completely intimidated by how flexible everyone was. I was very strong and fast but so tight I couldn't even touch my toes. Then the instructor had us do a headstand. This was my first class! And I had a stress fracture. I wasn't sure I should even try it, but I didn't have the energy to resist. I just went along with it and hoped for the best. I managed to get my legs up and didn't feel discomfort in my back, but I did feel as if my brain was going to ooze out of the top of my head. So many thoughts swirled in my mind: *This is not for me . . . I can't do this . . . I'm not made for this . . . I'm not bendy; there's no way . . .*

The instructor must have noticed how much I was struggling because she came over to me, looked me in the eyes, and said, "Breathe with me." She took a deep inhale. I inhaled with her, and then we both exhaled together. It felt so good. I don't think I'd taken a deep inhale or exhale since I'd felt that sharp pain. In that moment, I felt at peace. A tingling sensation spread across my body. And I remembered: that was the feeling I'd had when I was baptized as a child. That was the Holy Spirit! I was amazed. I felt a connection with Spirit for the first time since my injury.

From that moment, yoga became my best friend. I started going to class regularly, and slowly, my muscles relaxed and my yoga improved. Breathing deeply during my practice, I continued to feel connected to Spirit. My stress and anxiety levels dropped. I felt better enough to start swimming and biking to help my body strengthen and recover. After six months, I felt lighter, more optimistic, and more confident. My body was fit and powerful. Healthier mentally, spiritually, and physically, I was able to return to the track a year after my injury. I went on to win three championship titles in the high jump, heptathlon, and mile relay and to lead Wichita State to their first Women's Track and Field Championship title. All because of yoga.

When I got injured, I was so afraid: afraid of being a failure, afraid of being judged, afraid of who I'd be without track. By opening myself up to change, I discovered yoga and my capacity to heal and adapt. I was able to come back stronger and thrive in a completely unexpected way.

For me, a potentially career-ending track injury ignited my fears. For you, it may be a job loss, divorce, death of a loved one, or any type of setback that leaves you anxiously wondering, *What now?* Most fears boil down to one of these four types:

- Fear of failure
- Fear of judgment
- Fear of change
- Fear of being the first

Let's take a look at each of these types of fear from a love-based mind-set instead of a fear-based one, revealing the opportunity in each of them.

Before You Begin

I invite you to start practicing personal self-care right away, even as you read through these pages. Use my morning, afternoon, and nighttime wellness routines as inspiration. Pick two to three practices suggested below that resonate with you, and feel free to try different ones each day. There are no rules in this book, only suggestions. So mix it up! Don't worry if you don't understand what a term means or how to do each practice. I'll explain everything over the course of the book. There are plenty of options here to get you started, including taking a walk or drinking lime water. Practice for the length of time that works for you. I like to meditate for 20 minutes each morning, but you may prefer 5 minutes. Developing a consistent practice of self-care is what's most important.

Morning Routine (6 A.M. to 8 A.M.)

- Write my morning pages
- Say my affirmations
- Meditate for 20 minutes
- Say my gratitude prayer
- Look at the water, look at the horizon during sunrise
- Drink lime water (2 tablespoons of lime juice in 16 ounces of water) with a pinch of cayenne pepper
- Do yoga for 30 minutes, usually beginning with Sun Salutations A and B
- Visualize my ideal day
- Walk or run one mile
- Take a cool shower
- Eat breakfast of a superfood smoothie or juice or a fruit plate with three to five of my favorite fruits

Afternoon Routine (12 P.M. to 2 P.M.)

- Drink 16 ounces of lime water with a pinch of cayenne pepper
- Meditate for 20 minutes
- Eat a superfood salad with three to five of my favorite veggies
- Midday Dance (#DanceDaily)

Nighttime Routine (9 P.M. to 11 P.M.)

- Write in my gratitude journal for 20 minutes
- Meditate for 20 minutes
- Do yin yoga for 20 minutes
- Read an inspirational book
- Say affirmations

THE FEAR OF FAILURE: KEEP GOING, KEEP GROWING

The most common fear is a fear of failure. We all fear not being good enough. Not being good enough to start a new business, or take a class, or try something new. If you let it, fear of failure will keep you from trying, period. And it will keep you from doing your best. You won't give 100 percent because you're too afraid of giving your all and failing. Instead, you won't put very much effort in at all . . . because then, if it doesn't work out, it's not as if you really put yourself out there anyway, right?

If you are afraid to fail so much that you don't even try, then you are holding yourself back.

Don't be afraid to take a risk.

Don't be afraid to follow your dreams and your heart.

If you are passionate about a project or new venture, go for it. If it doesn't work out, you'll use that experience to learn, grow, and get stronger.

One of the most valuable lessons my dad taught me was to follow my dreams and to be persistent. If I didn't achieve my dream on the first try, then he'd encourage me to try again. He'd always say, "Keep going; keep trying; never give up." It doesn't matter if you're first or if you're last as long as you're headed toward the finish line.

I tell myself, "You don't fail until you stop trying."

If you have a goal and you're moving forward and getting closer to realizing it, then you're not failing. There may be some setbacks along the way. It may not be a straight path to the finish line, but with each obstacle, with each challenge, you're growing and getting stronger.

Once we look at those situations that challenge us as opportunities for growth, then we can never fail. You have to think, *This challenge is not me failing. This is me getting stronger.*

The Fear of Judgment: Put Yourself Out There

I was bashed along with others on social media because I'd chosen to work with a company that was accused of behaving badly. Lots of people said I should sever my ties with them and criticized me for my decision not to. Anger-filled messages came from every corner. I didn't budge or go low. I was confident in my choice, and I stood up for myself, my friends who had also decided to keep working with the company, and my community of followers who supported me. I would not have been able to do that a couple of years ago. Back then, I was too scared—scared I would get hurt if I spoke up, scared I wouldn't say the right things. Back then, the fear of judgment kept me quiet.

Today I know that I'm not always going to say the right things, and that's okay. I'm speaking up, making my voice heard, and that alone makes a difference. The goal isn't to be perfect. It's to make progress, to get better and better along the way. To put yourself out there regardless of what people think—and let the chips fall where they may.

> *Speak your truth—even when your voice shakes.*

Deciding which athletic scholarship for college to choose paralyzed me with indecision. What if I picked wrong? The stakes were high for me. This was the most important step toward my goals of getting a degree and qualifying for the Olympics. I was so afraid to choose. What if I didn't get along with the coach or the program didn't fit my needs? What if the other athletes were much better than me, and I flamed out and got cut from the team? What if I couldn't handle the academics and lost my scholarship? What would my friends and family say if I messed up this amazing opportunity? I could hear them already: "Why did you do that? That was so stupid." It was the most pressure I'd ever felt. Eventually, I had to make a decision, and I did.

We fear being judged for making the "wrong" decision just as much as we fear failure. But wrong to whom? Better to make a decision, even if it turns out to be the wrong decision for you, than to not make any decision at all. At least by making a decision, you're moving forward. If it turns out to be a mistake, you can learn from it. If you don't make a decision at all, you don't have a chance to grow.

Nothing is worse than having someone else make a decision for you. We are each unique spiritual beings. We each have a unique purpose in life. When you let someone else dictate what that purpose is, it's impossible to live your own truth. Advice, even if well meant, is really someone else telling you what's on their heart and soul. You're not living from your spiritual heart if you just mindlessly follow them. Don't let the fear of judgment take that away from you. Follow your heart.

yoga practice: child's pose

Child's Pose, one of the main relaxation poses in yoga, releases tension in your neck, shoulders, and back and calms the nervous system. Even if you don't have a regular yoga routine, practicing this pose will help release the stress and anxiety your fears may be causing.

- Sit on your heels.
- Bring your feet together with your knees hip-width apart.
- Bend forward with an exhale, and rest your torso between your thighs.
- Relax your tailbone toward your feet.
- Reach your arms far forward.
- Spread your fingers, and relax your palms into the floor. Rest your forehead on the floor.
- Hold the pose and take 5 to 10 slow, deep breaths.
- Rise with an inhale.
- Exhale to relax.

THE FEAR OF CHANGE: OPEN YOURSELF UP TO NEW DREAMS

Sometimes things are changing and we don't even realize it. When I got injured and then healed myself through yoga and a greater connection to Spirit, I didn't realize immediately that my life was changing. I thought, *Thank you yoga for helping me, but now I can get back on the track and start running again.* I went right back to training hard for the next conference. I went right back to what was comfortable. It wasn't until a few years later that I realized I was stuck in a routine that wasn't serving me anymore. When I got injured again, I remembered how much yoga had helped me and how much of a blessing it was in my life, connecting me to my soul, helping me to make clearer decisions, and relieving my stress.

I was starting to realize I needed to change course. Track injuries were wearing down my body and wearing me out emotionally. I was burning out. A consistent yoga practice helped me to heal again and to eventually recognize that an Olympic win was an old dream. Somewhere along the way, a new dream had taken root: to better understand the magic of yoga. Opening myself up to that new dream changed my whole life and career path. It was a frightening time, going from thinking track would be my entire life to working toward becoming a yoga teacher and health and wellness coach. But once I let my new dream in, it flourished and crowded out any doubts I had about ending my track training. It felt right immediately. The truth is, the heart and soul of my dream—to be a positive role model—didn't change. The only thing that changed was *how* I'd be that positive role model.

I can vividly remember my dad telling my younger self that I was going to be a teacher. "No way!" I said. "Teaching is boring!" I'm giggling to myself now because I'm living a more adventurous life as a teacher than I could ever have imagined as a competitive athlete, and I'm loving every minute of it. I've even learned to embrace the challenges, haters, and accidents that go along with my new career. They are all a part of my growth and evolution to be the best version of myself, and they help keep me open to new dreams.

The only constant thing in life is change. If you're not changing, then you're not growing, and if you're not growing, you're dying. To be alive is to be open to, and flow with, the way things are shifting and changing.

As long as I'm breathing,
I'll never give up on myself.

meditation practice

Meditation helps me to listen and connect with my authentic self. The more I go within, the more I see the direction of my heart and the more I'm guided. In the quiet and stillness, my soul speaks volumes about the way I need to flow in the world, how I should move, and where I need to go. I encourage you to go within to work things out. The more you go within, the more you will be guided.

If meditation is new to you, I recommend practicing for five to ten minutes each day. Don't get frustrated if you have a hard time sitting in a calm position for that length of time. It's totally normal to be antsy. It will take some time for you to get used to being in complete silence and not let thoughts rule your brain. Be patient and keep with it. Try meditating first thing in the morning, when your mind is calm and fresh after a good night's sleep.

If you meditate regularly, I recommend a 20-minute practice, ideally twice a day.

There is a Zen teaching that says, "The most important thing is remembering the most important thing." Before you meditate, it's helpful to set an intention, or what matters to you most at that time, and focus your attention on it. The intention I've suggested for this meditation is to ease anxiety.

For this meditation, embrace these affirmations to set your intention: *I am patient with myself and others as truth and love reveal themselves through me daily. I understand that life is a cycle and everything has a process. I breathe peace and calmness into every cell of my body. I change all of the things that I can to align myself with love and accept all of the things that I cannot change. I allow people to find their own path to love.*

Now find a comfortable, quiet spot. You may want to set a timer to prevent yourself from worrying about the time elapsed. Then begin.

1. Sit comfortably. Find a spot that gives you a stable, solid, comfortable seat so that you feel relaxed.

2. Set your intention.

3. Notice what your legs are doing. If you're on the floor or a cushion, cross your legs comfortably in front of you. If on a chair, rest the bottoms of your feet on the floor.

4. Straighten your upper body—but don't stiffen. Your spine has a natural curvature. Let it be there.

5. Notice what your arms are doing. Situate your upper arms parallel to your upper body. Rest the palms of your hands on your legs, lap, or knees, wherever feels most natural.

6. Soften your gaze. Drop your chin a little, and let your gaze fall gently downward. It's not necessary to close your eyes. You can simply let what appears before your eyes be there without focusing on it.

7. Feel your breath. Bring your attention to the physical sensation of breathing: the air moving through your nose or mouth.

8. Notice when your mind wanders from your breath. Inevitably, your attention will leave the breath and wander to other places. Don't worry. There's no need to block or eliminate thinking. When you notice your mind wandering, gently return your attention to the breath.

9. Be kind about your wandering mind. You may find your mind wandering constantly—that's normal too. Instead of wrestling with your thoughts, practice observing them without reacting. Just sit and pay attention. As hard as it may seem, that's all there is to it. Come back to your breath over and over again, without judgment or expectation.

10. When you're ready, gently lift your gaze (if your eyes are closed, open them). Take a moment and notice any sounds in the environment. Notice how your body feels right now. Notice your thoughts and emotions.

THE FEAR OF BEING THE FIRST: BE OUT IN FRONT

Moving to California, thousands of miles away from my close-knit family, was a big decision for me. I didn't know a soul out there. I wouldn't have family or friends to fall back on if things got tough. I wouldn't have people to talk to or spend time with. No one would know my name or who I was. It was scary, but I decided to do it anyway. I could have stayed close to family and friends. I could have stayed comfortable—it's always easier to stay comfortable—but I knew in my soul this move was the right next step for me.

If your soul is guiding you somewhere, follow it. If you have to go alone, go. Going it alone scares most people. We think, *Let me take a friend,* or *Let me go where the whole crowd is going.* But sometimes the place where you need to go is empty. No one is there yet. It's waiting for you to show up. You have to be the leader. You have to be the first.

Don't be afraid to lead.

Don't be afraid to be the first.

Don't be afraid to break the mold.

Too often we rely on people who have gone before us to show us the way. *Let me find out how they did it so I can do it that way too,* we think. Instead, be the one to break the mold. Find your own way. Be out front, and set the precedent for those who are coming up behind you. Be fierce.

TAKE AN INVENTORY

When's the last time you checked in with yourself and took an inventory of your life? It's easy to get caught up in the day-to-day, but it's important to pause and reflect on the big picture and make sure you're on the right path. If things are great, celebrate and make new life goals. If things aren't as great, it might be time to make a few changes. Take a moment now and reflect on four areas of your life.

On a scale of 1 to 10, with 10 being the most positive, think about how you would rate these parts of your life:

Health	1	2	3	4	5	6	7	8	9	10
Relationships	1	2	3	4	5	6	7	8	9	10
Career	1	2	3	4	5	6	7	8	9	10
Spirituality	1	2	3	4	5	6	7	8	9	10

Which areas need some work? Think about your answers as you do the rest of the practices in this book. They will help you better understand the fear that may be holding you back in that area so that you can set goals for yourself and find more balance. We'll take another inventory later on to see how things have changed.

Now list three of your fears. They can be as specific as "I'm afraid of starting a new job" or as general as "I'm afraid of failure." Naming your fears is the first step to owning and facing them. Think about this list as you read the book and use the practices to help you overcome the power these fears have over you.

1. I'm afraid of _____

_____

2. I'm afraid of _____

_____

3. I'm afraid of _____

_____

Remember: Be Strong

It takes courage to face your fears. I know it's not easy. Doing this work can dig up a lot of stuff you'd probably like to leave buried. But ignoring your fears or being blind to them allows them to fester and, ultimately, take over your life. You've already started shifting your mind-set about fear and are singling out the ones giving you trouble. Fears show us the places where we have room to grow. Once you identify them, you can learn from them, challenge them, and release them. You have the strength to do it. I know you do. You are much, much more than your fears.

affirmation practice

Say this affirmation several times upon waking in the morning and before going to bed at night:

I release everything that blocks me from my greatness.

CHAPTER TWO

From Pain to Power

After I pushed past the stress fracture in my back and had an amazing, winning sophomore year of college, I knew that I wanted to keep training and go all the way to the Olympics. I dreamt of winning a gold medal so that, as a recognizable Olympic athlete, I could make a positive difference in the world. When I graduated from college, I was ranked 13th in the nation and knew I had some work to do to be accepted to the track and field residence program at the Chula Vista Olympic Training Center in California. I was determined and ambitious. I cold-called a well-known coach at San Diego State. He did not know what to make of me at first!

"How did you get my number? How do I know you?" he asked.

"You don't know me, but I looked you up, and I need your help to get into the Olympic Training Center. The only thing I can promise you is that I'll get better every single day you work with me," I replied.

"I don't know who you are," he said, "but I like you, and I'll train you."

That was the only yes I needed to buy a plane ticket.

On my own and working hard to support myself, I pushed myself to the limit. Each day, I worked as a personal trainer from 5 A.M. to 10 A.M. and then ran track from 11 A.M. to 3 P.M.

I took a little break to eat and rest, and then it was back to the gym to work with clients from 5 P.M. to 10 P.M. I had a full roster of clients—and a waiting list. I was good at helping people achieve their fitness goals, whether it was to lose weight, gain weight, or build muscle and endurance. It was rewarding work and I loved doing it . . . but working that hard and training that hard wasn't a good match. I was stressed out, physically and emotionally. My eye was twitching. My hair was turning gray. And then I pulled my hamstring.

This injury gave me an opportunity to take a break and figure things out. I took a hard look at my life, goals, and level of happiness. And for the first time, the cons of running track and pursuing my dream of competing in the Olympics outweighed the pros.

So I stopped.

I realized I needed yoga again. It had helped me get through a really tough time before, a time of self-doubt and uncertainty, and I turned to it once more. I saw a yoga teacher training course being offered and decided that the more I knew about yoga, the more I'd be inspired and motivated to keep it up. So I registered, and it's one of the best things I've ever done in my life. I loved doing the asanas (postures) and the breath work, but the real change came once I learned about the spiritual aspects of yoga. After that, I knew that I was detoxing and aligning with my spiritual self.

Meditation also became a part of my life during my yoga training. At first, I was very uncomfortable. We had to sit in lotus position (which was very painful for me at the time), close our eyes, and listen to our breath. I peeked many times to see if anyone was in as much pain as I was. I always wondered if I was doing it right and exactly what it was I was supposed to feel. My mind would race from one thing to the next, first going through my day, then visualizing random things. But with each meditation, I felt less pain and more calm. That calm would stay with me throughout the day. Ending my day with meditation even helped me sleep better.

This time, yoga helped me heal and refocus, and it opened the door to a new life and way to share my gifts with the world. Today, I make a positive difference in the world as a yoga teacher and health coach rather than as an Olympic athlete.

Your past does not define your future. You can always change and move forward in a different way. Don't let your past haunt you—or define you.

Who you've been in the past is not who you have to be going forward.

The choices you've made in the past do not define your future. You can always make different choices right now.

The "failures" you've had in the past don't define your future—or mean you are going to "fail" again. You have the power to change the course of your life.

Create Your Future

Each moment, you have the power to create your future. Each moment, you have the power to define who you are, what you want, and how to get there. Every day, remind yourself: I am not going to let my past define me. I am going to define me. I am going to create my future.

Let go of the past and shape a future of your own making by:

- Getting comfortable being uncomfortable.
- Stretching yourself.
- Finding the love.
- Never calling it failure.

Get Comfortable Being Uncomfortable

Change is uncomfortable. But the only constant in life is change. Everything in nature changes. Trees change. Mountains change. Weather changes. The world around us—our relationships, jobs, living situations, friends, everything—is constantly changing and influencing us. Amid all of this change, why would we expect ourselves to stay the same? We're constantly changing. Honor that.

The scariest time in my life was when I realized my heart's desire had changed and I no longer wanted to run track. A lot of people feel that a change of heart is a negative thing. That it reflects a fickle nature. It doesn't. You don't have to prove yourself to anybody. You have to find what fits for *you*—right now, at this time in your life.

When we don't honor the ways in which we've changed, we end up sticking with something just because we don't want to quit. We end up stressed, overworked, and miserable, holding on for dear life to a dream we don't even want anymore. We're in a super-vulnerable position, hanging off the side of a cliff with no road in sight. This is dangerous—but as long as you're still breathing, as long as you're still alive, you have the opportunity to change your situation, haul yourself back on a path, and find a dream that's worth the gamble.

Each breath is an opportunity to change.

Each breath is an opportunity to be better than we were before.

With each breath we choose our future.

yoga practice:
crescent lunge release

- Stand in lunge position: step one leg forward with knee bent and come on to the toes of the back foot.

- Inhale as you sweep your arms above your head and exhale as you sweep your arms down by your sides.

- When you inhale, think of embracing love, and when you exhale, think of releasing fear.

STRETCH YOURSELF

The lessons I've learned on my yoga mat about flexibility help me practice flexibility in my life. Remember how I was so tight at my first yoga class that I couldn't even touch my toes? The body is often naturally tight, and that's okay. Breathe into your muscles, and they will get looser. The same thing happens in life. Breathe into your fears, and they will loosen their grip on you, opening you up to new opportunities. The more you breathe into your fears, the easier it gets to do so and the more flexible you will become in trying new things.

Change is happening all around us and inside of us. If you're flexible, you're able to move easily with those changes and find your flow. If you're not, you'll get stuck, unable to shift and adapt, and live in a way that isn't working for you anymore.

On the yoga mat, we learn to keep moving. In life, the more flexible you are and the more you keep moving, the less likely you are to get stuck in your fears, doubts, and worries.

Finding your balance on your mat can help you find balance in life.

Ocean Breathing Pranayama

The Sanskrit word *pranayama* comes from the roots *prana* (life energy, or the breath) and *yama* (to control). The way you think, move, and, most importantly, breathe contributes to the flow and vitality of your life force energy, the universal energy that runs through you and everything around you. Pranayama exercises are breathing exercises that can clear physical and emotional blockages in your body caused by daily stressors, trauma, and unhealthy habits. They allow your life force energy to flow freely. When your energy is flowing easily, you will feel energized and relaxed.

- Sit in a comfortable position. Lengthen your spine.
- Rest your hands on your knees. Close your eyes.
- Open your mouth. As you exhale, contract your throat and make a *hhhaaa* sound, as if you were fogging a mirror. It should sound like a soft whisper.

- Now close your mouth and breathe through your nose only, but continue to make this *hhhaaa* sound with each inhale and exhale.
- Repeat 10 rounds of this breath.

Modification: Place a firm cushion or rolled mat under your bottom to bring more length to your spine and release pressure on your knees.

FIND THE LOVE

When I was a child, my mom told me, "Whatever you do, do it in love." My household was very strict, so it wasn't always easy to be happy, but my mom would regularly ask me, "Are you happy? If you're not happy, you can always stop." Sometimes I replied that I was happy, but other times I'd admit, "Yeah, I'm not happy right now. I need to take a breather and find the love in what I'm doing."

If there's no love in your actions, you won't be happy or succeed. The fun goes out of the experience. There's usually not much love when people push themselves too far, as during the end of my track and field training. Until I got injured, I hadn't checked in with myself and asked, "Wait a minute. Am I having fun here? If I'm not, why not?" If you're miserable, it's time to take a step back, take a break, and try to find the love again. And if the love isn't there, move on to something else. You won't get the results you want if the love isn't there.

When I first went vegetarian and then vegan, I was so excited about eating a plant-based diet and buying ingredients in bulk to save money that I'd make enough food for myself and for my neighbors. This turned into selling food out of my house—and then to people calling me a chef because the food was that good. My popularity grew, and I started booking jobs as a personal chef and catering events. I loved cooking flavorful, healthy meals, and I was making a nice income for myself doing it, but food and nutrition was only one part of the health-coaching business I was trying to get off of the ground. Although I'd be hired as a cook for a client, I would start life coaching and health coaching them as well. We'd meditate and do some yoga. That holistic approach was more in alignment with what I believe about wellness: it's not just about eating nutrient-rich food; it's about nourishing your mind and body.

There came a point where I didn't want to cook anymore. I didn't want to be known as a chef; I wanted to be known as a coach and a guide. When I checked in with myself, I realized the fun had gone, and I couldn't let my past success define me any longer. It was too limiting and didn't reflect who I was or who I wanted to be. I needed to find a new way. I stopped taking food-centric jobs and focused on developing clients interested in all that I had to offer. It wasn't easy turning down gigs, especially on my bank account, but it was worth it to do what felt good in my heart and soul.

It takes guts to realize something doesn't feel good on a soul level anymore and to make a change. Oftentimes, we hold back because we're scared to disappoint our clients, family, and friends. We think, *I can't quit my job to start a new business. I have a family to feed,* or *My family expects me to continue the legacy of the family business. There's no way I can start a different career.* We get stuck believing that we have to do what others think we're good at. Just because everyone oohs and aahs over the latest dress you made, it doesn't mean you have to be a clothing designer. If you don't feel the passion in it, don't do it. Follow your heart to find the love.

I found the love in fitness competitions for a while. They gave me the incentive to put more effort into my exercise and a reason to be my fittest self. Beating someone else didn't drive me, but doing my best did. In my first competition, I entered the fitness model category and had a blast on that stage. I worked my cute outfits, rocked to my stellar playlist, and had such a great time. The judges could tell I was enjoying myself and commented on my charisma. And I won!

Then it was time for the figure competition. I hadn't planned on entering because I didn't think I had enough muscle, but one judge was cheering me on so hard that I decided, Why not? I was feeling so good, I'd keep it rolling. I got up on that stage in my bikini, flexed my muscles, stuck out my booty, and did my thing, smiling wide. When they announced me as the winner, no one was more surprised than I was. The other women looked confused, and I bet for a second I did too. But then I was so filled with excitement and gratitude. I have no doubt what won it: I'd found the love. I deserved to win because my heart and soul was in it, and that was a beautiful thing.

But after that competition, my motivation became more about trying to win than about feeling the love—and it showed in the results. Now there was tension and anxiety. My vibe was totally different, and I knew I needed to leave competitions behind. It's so easy to get caught up in pushing yourself that you lose sight of why you are doing so in the first place. Love always needs to be in the lead.

I follow my heart and trust that it will eventually lead me to where I need to be.

REALITY CHECK

Is what you're doing—your job, friendships, how you spend your time—making you happy? Make a list of the pros and cons. Are the pros outweighing the cons? If so, you're probably on the right path. Have the cons taken over? Dig a little deeper. Are you bored? Did someone or something hurt you? Or do you really feel that this endeavor doesn't reflect who you are anymore? It's not always immediately clear what you should do, but the act of acknowledging the benefits and drawbacks of your current path and writing them down will help you to make a decision. You don't have to change course just because the cons outweigh the pros, but it's a signal to look within yourself and determine if it's really something you want to move forward with.

meditation practice

Follow the numbered meditation instructions on pages 14–15 and use the following as your intention:

I release everything that blocks me from my greatness. I am ready to live in love and release fear every time it shows up in my life. I let go of relationships that don't serve my greatest good.

NEVER CALL IT FAILURE

Things don't always work out the way we want or plan. When a deal falls through, a client goes to a competitor, a job opportunity vanishes, a relationship ends, a proposal is rejected, or an experience falls short of your expectations, don't call it a failure. Call it an opportunity. Shift your mind-set. Stop asking, *How did I fail? How can I stop failing?* Rather, start asking, *How did that situation make me stronger? What can I learn from that experience?*

When I'm at the gym lifting weights and I can't lift the weight I'd set as my goal for that day, I don't think, *Oh, man, I failed.* I think, *That's my limit now. Time to let my body rest and recover.* I'll go back to the gym the next day and try again, even stronger. It's about mind-set. It's about not calling it failure.

Here again, it's important to do a reality check. Do you want to keep pursuing this goal, or do you want to stop? Ask yourself: *Is this something I want to push forward, or do I want to completely let it go and put my energy into another direction? Am I happy on this journey?*

If you decide to move ahead, realize that you won't fail unless you stop trying. If you're enjoying the journey, you're moving in the right direction. You are going toward the finish line, and you will eventually succeed.

If you dislike the journey more than you like it, you should put your time, energy, and resources into pursuing a different course.

Every setback is an opportunity to grow.

What is one thing you can do *today* to change the trajectory of your future?

_____

_____

Remember: Clean the Slate

At any moment, you can give yourself a clean slate and move forward into the future with confidence:

I am not going to let my past define me.

I am not going to let past decisions, mistakes, or setbacks define me.

I am going to define me.

Each moment, I am going to create my future.

affirmation practice

Say this affirmation several times upon waking
in the morning and before going to bed at night:

*I am ready to heal any place within me holding
on to residual fear from past experiences.*

CHAPTER THREE

You're Not a Victim— You're a Creator

Not many people know this, but I've been sexually assaulted more times than I'd like to remember.

The first time, I was in high school, and it was my best friend who hurt and betrayed me. I never told my parents or friends and basically tried to pretend as if it hadn't happened. I broke up with my boyfriend at the time because I didn't feel worthy of him anymore, and I decided to stay close to home for college even though I had scholarship offers from great schools across the country and my plan had been to spread my wings and go far away. Fear started to take over my life.

Food was my comfort. Instead of gaining the freshman 15, I gained 25 pounds in my first three months of college. My athletic performance suffered big-time. With the extra weight, I was getting slower and slower on the track. I went from jumping 5'10" to not even being able to clear 5'4". My confidence took a deep dive. I worried about losing my scholarship. I was absolutely miserable. My coaches knew I was struggling but didn't understand what was going on with me, and I didn't tell them. I kept quiet and prayed for God to help me heal and show me a way out of the darkness, a way to trust myself again and regain my self-esteem. These were dark days, and part of me doesn't even know how I managed to get through them. Later that year, my assistant coach threw me a lifeline when he told me he was taking a new job at Wichita State and suggested I transfer there to train with him. It was a chance to start over. "You need a clean slate," he said. I agreed.

The new environment helped a lot. I channeled my energy into training and practicing and got back into shape. My times started improving, and my confidence was boosted. I probably looked pretty good on the outside, but inside I was still raw and hurt. I closed that part of myself off from others and tried to move forward with my life as best I could. Only when yoga, meditation, and a regular spirituality practice entered my life did I feel as if I was able to process the assault and eventually heal. It took a long, long time.

But much of that healing was stripped away when I was date-raped a few years after the initial assault. Again, I was betrayed by someone close to me, someone whom I trusted. I was devastated. How could a person who liked me or valued me do something like this to me? I felt ashamed, disrespected, and disregarded. Fear consumed me again. During the attack I disconnected from my body, and I never felt the same in my skin again. I went years without feeling desire or sensuality. I didn't want a romantic relationship or to express my sexuality in any way. None. Zero. I felt nothing. I thought I was broken, and friends thought I was weird. I wondered if I'd ever be able to experience and enjoy sex again.

Eventually, I said to myself, *Koya, you have to figure this out*. I knew I couldn't do it alone. It took many different life coaches to help me to work through my anger and resentment and to forgive. The teachings of Lisa Nichols, Louise Hay, Marianne Williamson, Iyanla Vanzant, Michael Bernard Beckwith, and Neale Donald Walsch helped me to release my pain and believe that I am worthy and I am love, no matter what happens to me. The work rebuilt my self-esteem and confidence, but not my desire.

I couldn't understand why it hadn't returned. I wasn't holding on to the anger anymore, so why hadn't the switch flipped? The only answer was to just let it go.

It was being loved and allowing myself to be loved that eventually made me whole. It took over a year of dating a kind, patient, loving man before I trusted men again. Being nurtured in this way was what I needed to heal the trauma of my rapes, and I think the universe knew that.

Flash forward over a decade. After all of this work and healing, after becoming a personal coach myself, how is it possible that I could be assaulted again? I asked myself this over and over in the days and months following my third assault. Again, by someone whom I knew and trusted. I had never imagined something like this could happen to me again. I told the universe, *Hey, I got through that part of my life—twice. I've learned all I need to know from these experiences.* In total shock, I wondered if I unconsciously draw this negative energy to me. *Wow, wow, wow,* I thought. *How is this possible?*

All I wanted to do was move forward. The inner well of strength I'd cultivated through my training over the years would be enough to sustain me. There was way too much going on in my life, and I didn't have the time to press pause and deal with this new rape. I went to the doctor to check for STDs, but that was it. After that, I lived as if the assault hadn't happened. I cared for my sick auntie, taught workshops, mentored private clients, and prepared for an upcoming yoga teacher training. I was exhausted in mind and body nurturing everyone else around me and ignoring myself, but I kept going and going and going. After my previous experiences, I knew I *could* heal—but I wasn't actually doing the work of healing. I probably would have kept on that way until I broke down if it hadn't been for a brave woman who shared her story.

We were both participating in a sharing circle, a small gathering of women where we held space for one another and allowed each participant to express whatever was on her mind to the group, like a fear, limiting belief, or personal story, without judgment or feedback. We just listened and accepted. When it was this young woman's turn, she revealed that she'd recently been raped and had disconnected from her body.

Hearing her express what I'd also felt compelled me to share my own story for the first time. Everyone in the circle who knew me was shocked. And it *was* shocking. I had hidden my pain well. But I wanted to reassure this young woman that she wasn't alone, she didn't have to go through her healing alone, and that no matter what happened to her physical body, nothing could touch her soul. In saying my story and these truths out loud to a community of supportive women, I started my own healing.

I share these experiences with you because I know firsthand how important and powerful it is to bring our stories out of the darkness and into the light. And I want you to know that I don't take healing from trauma lightly. Maybe you've been assaulted, battered, or traumatized in some way. Our circumstances may be different, but we share a pain and, more importantly, the capacity to grow from pain. We do this when we look our fear in the face, decide not to live with a victim mind-set, and embrace— heart and soul—our power as creators.

YOU ARE A CREATOR

A victim is a person harmed, injured, or killed as a result of a crime, accident, or other event or action. When you approach life with a victim mind-set, you believe things happen to you, that you have no control, especially over your future. When you approach life with a creator mind-set, you believe you have the power to *create* your future and to use negative experiences to make yourself and others stronger.

After I was abused in high school, I identified with the victim mind-set. I lived in the past, revisiting this traumatic experience every day, and let it shape my future. Fearful and distrustful of others, especially guys, I didn't want to date or be in a relationship. Closing myself off was easier. The second assault provoked those feelings all over again but even more intensely. Looking for ways to mend, I spoke with renowned life coaches, took courses at the Agape Spiritual Center, and immersed myself in inspirational and spiritual teachings. The turning point came when I realized the only way I would heal and create a new future for myself was by shifting from a victim mind-set to a creator mind-set. Every day, I told myself over and over again, "I am not a victim; I am a creator." It took a while for me to believe it, but the supportive community I'd found and books such as *A Course in Miracles* by Helen Schucman and *Conversations with God* by Neale Donald Walsch provided the footing I needed to start making the shift.

Once I realized that I could create beauty around me even as I was feeling pain inside, the shift was complete. I could be a good friend and daughter. I could share my creativity and talents by making delicious, nourishing meals for my loved ones and raising my voice in song. There was positive energy in me.

When I met a man who seemed nice enough to take a risk on, I was ready. I thought, *I'm going to see what kind of relationship I'll have with this person if I release my fears. I'm going to enjoy him for who he is. He has nothing to do with the past. What if I just enjoyed and trusted him?* I changed my story, and we ended up having a beautiful relationship. Love carried me over the line, but it was my inner strength as a creator that got me to the field.

A creator takes a traumatic experience and uses it to become stronger. She doesn't allow it to keep hurting her but rather takes something terrible and turns it into something beautiful. I am a stronger person because of the abuse that happened to me. I took a different route to get to that strength in each instance, and some routes were a lot longer and more circuitous than I would have liked, but I got there. And a key turning point on my journey was recognizing myself as a creator, capable of shaping my future.

I'm not saying that by definition you are not a victim. If someone abused you, you are a victim of abuse. But if you keep living your life as if you'll never get back on your feet because of that abuse, then you are carrying your victimhood into the future and approaching life with a victim mind-set. You are choosing to remain a victim. Or you can choose to be a creator and consider, *How can I use what happened to me to make me stronger? How can I use what happened to me to help other people heal and thrive?*

Victim Mind-Set
Because this happened to me . . .
I started taking drugs.
I gave up on life.

I _____

Creator Mind-Set
Because this happened to me . . .
I am now doing what I love.
I know how to set boundaries.

I _____

Everything around us, including you, is made of energy vibrating at different frequencies. When your vibration is high, you are connected to your authentic self and filled with love, joy, compassion, and gratitude. You attract more positive energy. When your vibration is low, you are filled with fear or negative emotions such as shame, guilt, sadness, and anger and draw more of the same. At a low vibration, you'll find it tough to align with your heart and soul. Your dreams seem to be out of reach.

A victim mind-set lowers your vibration and attracts more negative energy—more and more of what you don't want. You might attract people who support victimhood and are stuck in the negative experiences of the past. It's okay to tell the story of a traumatic experience, and this is necessary to process it. But it's easy to get stuck in your story, allowing it to define you, by sharing it over and over with no forward movement. When you're stuck like that, not growing or changing, you're dying. There is nothing worse than being stuck in a situation that brings you down, brings you pain, and doesn't make you feel good. Get unstuck by shifting to a creator mind-set and raising your vibration.

LIVING AS A CREATOR

Once you think, *this tragic situation happened to me and I can move beyond it*, you've become a creator.

Yes, it's that easy and instantaneous.

As soon as you decide that what happened to you in the past is not something you want to carry into your future, you become a creator.

As soon as you decide that you are not a victim, you become a creator.

Living as a creator isn't always easy. It's important to support your new mind-set in the following ways:

- Prioritize Self-Care
- Take Full Responsibility for Your Feelings
- Forgive and Let Go
- Surround Yourself with Positive People
- Share Your Story

Prioritize Self-Care

To be a creator, you must value yourself. You must love yourself. Show how much by prioritizing self-care. Self-care is not selfish. It's a necessary practice that helps us be our best selves. When we love ourselves first, we are then able to show up more present and compassionate to others and the planet. Prioritize you: your healing, your joy, your wellness, your peace. How do you plan to spend today loving up on yourself?

Nurture any place in your life that needs more love.

If you want flowers, buy them. If you want a massage, go get one. If you want to take an evening walk, get out there. If you want to go the movies, buy a ticket. Eat foods that support your health and well-being. Hang out with friends who cherish you. Love yourself enough to make time and space to do the things that make you feel good and raise your vibration. And get comfortable doing these activities by yourself as well as with a friend or in a group. So often, we don't do fun things unless we do them with another person. Your self-care is worth more than any mild discomfort you may feel flying solo.

Fill Your Love Bank

Write down, or note on your phone, 5 to 10 people or things that bring you joy and make you smile. This is your Love Bank. My Love Bank is filled with a massage, a walk on the beach, a bubble bath, and playing with my nieces and nephews. When you feel sad, hurt, betrayed, attacked, or any other negative emotion, reach into your Love Bank. Help yourself to feel better by reminding yourself of the goodness and love that surrounds you. Love, like energy, can't be destroyed. It's only transferred. Negative emotions encourage more negative emotions. Love encourages more love. I choose love. How about you? Write down what you have in your Love Bank:

_____

_____

_____

_____

_____

Take Full Responsibility for Your Feelings

It's easy to slip back into a victim mind-set and blame others for how you feel. The teacher of one of my classes at Agape wouldn't let us shift the blame. Every time we tried to blame someone else for how we were feeling, my teacher would interrupt and say, "I." He would not let us say "they," as in "They made me feel angry" or "They made me feel sad." Rather, we had to say "I," as in "I feel angry" or "I feel sad." He would always remind us to take full responsibility for our feelings. When you take full responsibility, you affirm that you are responsible for your emotions and how you digest and process the situation. You are responsible for how your life moves forward. Pay attention to your language. Are you blaming others or taking responsibility?

Forgive and Let Go

We often think of forgiving and letting go as difficult tasks, but they don't have to be. We make them hard by convincing ourselves that the other party doesn't deserve to be forgiven and it's our job to punish them. The truth is, by not forgiving someone, we are punishing ourselves. By holding on to negative feelings, we can't move forward with our own lives.

I realize that not all situations are the same. Is it easier to forgive a stranger who cut you off in traffic than it is to forgive a boyfriend who cheated on you? Possibly. But forgiveness in any situation or circumstance requires the same shift in your perspective. Once you make that shift and practice using it, you will find it gets easier to forgive no matter what the reason. And bringing more forgiveness into your life will make you feel so much better.

The shift? Don't take things personally. If you were hit by a car, you would get mad at the person driving it, right? But what if the car didn't have a driver? You couldn't really blame anyone. Okay, maybe you could blame the manufacturer of the car, but getting back to the point. Forgiving someone doesn't mean you forget what they did to you or that you have to let them back into your life, but it's the first step to growing into a better version of yourself. *Koya*, you're thinking, *how can you not take rape personally? How can you forgive someone who assaulted you?* I don't take the assaults personally because they weren't about me. They were about the perpetrator. I couldn't control their actions, but I can control my response to them, and I choose forgiveness.

Forgiveness can lessen the grip traumatic events have on you and help you focus on other, more positive parts of your life. Forgiveness shows compassion for the one who hurt you. It doesn't justify what they did or remove their personal responsibility for their actions. Forgiveness releases your emotional pain and provides you with peace of mind. Forgiveness is good for *you*. Trust me.

The next step is to let go and release the control the person and situation may have had over your life. It is one thing to forgive, but if you don't let go, you will still feel like you can't move on with your life and keep on growing.

Practice letting go by thinking of yourself and what is best for you, and leave the hurtful person or situation in the past. It's important to be able to distinguish between what you still need in your life and what no longer serves you. We are all really good at accumulating things in our houses and people in our lives because we are afraid to lose things and people that we may need in the future. We're so good that our homes are bursting with clutter and unused stuff and our lives are filled with people who drain us. That's why it's so important to ask yourself, *Is holding on to this resentment serving me in some way? What do I need to let go of?*

If someone doesn't really give you anything but a headache, it's time to let go. Honor the good things this person may have brought you at one time, but accept that it is time to get him or her out of your life.

As you let go of grudges, you'll no longer define your life by how you've been hurt, and you'll open yourself up to people who give you what you really need. Try filling in these blanks if you're struggling to forgive someone:

I forgive _____

for _____

and I set myself free.

Then try this letting go visualization: Visualize yourself flying away from the situation like a dove gracefully hovering over the sea. If any residual emotion comes up, let it drop into the ocean to be washed away by the waves. Anytime a person or situation brings up negative emotions in me, I just send them out to sea.

Surround Yourself with Positive People

As soon as you decide to be a creator, you raise your vibration and start attracting more positive people into your life who are going to support your new lifestyle, your new way of thinking, and your new vibration. Unfortunately, toxic people may also be more attracted to you, like a moth to a flame (cue Janet Jackson singing "That's the Way Love Goes"). It's so important to separate yourself from energy vampires who only focus on the negative. Their negative energy will lower your vibration. You don't have to waste your time with energy vampires. Allow them to exhaust themselves and be consumed by their own fears. It's not your job to convince them of anything. Distance yourself from them and keep loving, keep shining.

Instead, surround yourself with people who are positive with a creator mind-set. Negative things happen to everyone. I'm not sending you to find people who are living the perfect life. I'm reminding you to value those people who understand that no matter what happens, we can heal and move forward as creators.

Share Your Story

By sharing your story, you open a space for other women to share theirs, and you invite love, nurture, and support into your life. It's taken me a long time to understand the importance of sharing. I know it's really hard to do. How can you share your story if you don't remember what happened or aren't entirely able to make sense of it? With trauma, nothing is clear. Self-judgment clouds our perceptions. Trying to hide or stay strong takes a toll.

I felt a huge release in my heart when I finally talked about a recent assault with a group of women. I felt the love and support of community. I'd need to lean on that love and support because the release and lightness I felt was soon followed by pain—the most massive, excruciating physical pain I'd ever felt in my life. I thought I was dying. Doubled over, clutching my middle, I finally agreed to go to the ER.

An ovarian cyst had ruptured, and on top of that, I had a bacterial infection. The doctors loaded me up with pain medication and antibiotics. I don't like taking drugs, especially pain medication, but I was willing to try anything. Sometimes the drugs worked, but a lot of times they didn't, and the only thing that eased my suffering was the care and concern of my friends and boyfriend. Now that they knew what was going on with me physically and emotionally because I'd told them of the assault, their nurturing was even more powerful. It meant so much to me to be so supported physically, emotionally, and spiritually as they prepared herbal tonics, prayed with me, and energetically ushered in my healing. Love has always played a role in helping me to heal, but this was something different, even more beautiful and profoundly transformational. Their care was the silver lining to my dark cloud of pain.

The mind and body are connected. I believe that cyst bursting was related to the release of my trauma. Who knows, if I'd kept that story inside of me, how big that cyst would have gotten and how much more life-threatening it could have been? And if I hadn't shared my story, I wouldn't have felt the full power of the healing love of my strong, supportive community.

You don't have to face traumatic situations alone. Reach out to your community, your loved ones, and let them know what's happening and how you're feeling. I didn't do that at first, but I know better now: there is power in sharing your story and revealing your truth.

yoga practice: chair pose release

- Stand with your feet together or hip-width apart, feet parallel.

- Reach your arms toward the sky with an inhale, palms facing each other.

- Bend your knees with an exhale and shift your hips back and down as if you were sitting on an imaginary chair.

- Make sure that your knees are not beyond your toes.

- Gaze diagonally downward.

- Hold the pose and take slow, deep breaths.

- Rise with an inhale, then exhale and release your arms by your side.

- Repeat 5 to 10 times.

Ask Yourself: How Can This Make Me Stronger?

If you are feeling like a victim in any area of your life, remember to ask yourself, *How can I turn these lemons into lemonade?*

Tough times are only moments, but they can last as long as we want them to. Every challenge is an opportunity for growth. We choose if we want to allow situations to make us bitter or better. It's not always easy to turn lemons into lemonade, but it's always possible. Be patient and kind with yourself as you use this book to find your own personal recipe for sweetening your life.

I am energy. I will change and shift,
but I will never be destroyed.
I am UNBREAKABLE.

meditation practice

People will try to tell you how you should process an experience. Maybe they've been in a similar situation and found a way that worked for them. That's great—for them. You have an inner guide, found in your soul and heart, that will show you your way. Use meditation to quiet your mind and tap in to it.

Follow the numbered meditation instructions on pages 14–15, and use the following as your intention:

I am ready to heal any place within me holding on to residual fear from past experiences. I am not a victim; I am a creator.

VISUALIZATION TO HEAL TRAUMA

Visualization, or mental imagery, has helped me in many ways, including healing from trauma. As an athlete, I've often used visualization to improve my performance. Research has shown that people who imagine themselves performing a task improve their performance in that task. It works because our brains interpret the thought as real-life action, priming the body to act in the same way we imagined. But visualization isn't just for athletes. It can help you to forgive, let go, and heal from trauma. Try this:

1. Clear your mind with a 5- to 10-minute meditation.

2. Visualize the person who hurt you.

3. Say "I forgive you for _____

_____ ."

4. Forgive yourself for holding on to the pain or anger, whether it was for 1 minute or over 20 years.

5. Repeat this practice daily until you feel peace of mind.

Tell someone close to you how you've healed. This is important because, if you cry or become angry when sharing, it's a sign you should keep repeating steps 1 through 5 or consider professional help.

Remember: Shine

We are spiritual beings having a human experience. Your physical body is not who you are; your spiritual self, or soul, is. No matter what happens to your physical body, nothing can touch your soul. Don't let the pain and trauma you have experienced hold you back from a future of your making. No matter how many times your heart is shattered, no matter how many times you're betrayed, you were meant to shine just like the sun. Breathe through the pain and come back stronger.

You're not a victim. You're a creator.

affirmation practice

Say this affirmation several times upon waking in the morning and before going to bed at night:

I am worthy of love, acceptance, and peace of mind.

CHAPTER FOUR

You Are Enough

I will never forget it. I was about 12 years old, belting "Ain't No Mountain High Enough" at the top of my lungs with the karaoke machine I got for Christmas, blessing the whole house with my vocals, when my dad yelled from the back room, "Koya, shut up!" His words stopped me cold. I'd never heard the words "shut up" pass his lips before. Never. I was so hurt by his language and his tone that I immediately burst into tears. In that moment, a sense that I shouldn't sing wiggled its way into my mind and ate at my confidence. I stopped singing in public. I was too afraid that my voice wasn't good enough and I'd be judged harshly.

I know now that my dad spoke out of frustration after a long week at work and just wanting some quiet. He didn't intend me any harm and certainly didn't want me to stop singing altogether. But that's what happened. I internalized the limiting belief that "my voice isn't good enough to share," and it took me a long time to recognize how it was holding me back. I had loved to sing, but once this limiting belief took hold, I went silent for years, too self-conscious to share my voice with the world. Once I identified this negative belief and challenged it, I was able to transform it from a limiting belief to a liberating belief. This new belief launched me forward to not only start singing again but to release my first single. Never silence your voice to comfort others. Be loud; be bold; be you!

LIVE FROM YOUR AUTHENTIC SELF

Limiting beliefs hold you in a place of fear and prevent you from hearing your heart, achieving your dreams, and becoming your best self. They will prevent you from moving forward and doing the things you want to do in life. I spent too much time allowing my limiting belief that "my voice isn't good enough to share" to silence the voice of my authentic self. In my heart and soul, I knew I was meant to share my passion and joy for singing, but I let this limiting belief win for a long time.

By challenging your own limiting beliefs, you will confront a common and potent type of fear and take a huge step toward reconnecting with your authentic self. Remember, your authentic self is your true self. When we honor our authentic selves and live from their guidance, we know our gifts, acknowledge our worth, and accept who we are *as we are*. When we are in alignment with our authentic selves we are filled with confidence, joy, and excitement. When we are out of alignment, we feel confused, anxious, depressed, and disempowered. When we live from our own unique, authentic place, we experience a fulfillment that feels like bliss, and we inspire people around us. If you aren't coming from a space of being authentically you, you won't feel happy on the inside. You will be constantly unfulfilled. Underneath layers and layers of limiting beliefs is your authentic self.

For a long time, my authentic self lived underneath a wig. I loved my wigs. I had a drawer filled with 30 of them! There's nothing wrong with wearing a wig, but there's something wrong if you don't love what's underneath it. And I didn't. I hated managing my natural hair, and when I started modeling, I thought I had to look a certain way to get booked for jobs.

Appearing on the cover of *Oxygen* magazine was my dream. Since I wasn't running track anymore, I thought modeling would be the way I could be a public figure and an inspiration for others, especially women of color, to live a healthy and active lifestyle. Getting on that cover would validate my new life and body. I was in great shape and sent in picture after picture with wig after wig. Four different wigs, four different cover tries, and I still didn't get picked. Eventually, I gave up, figuring that cover just wasn't for me.

Soon after, I checked myself on my hair. Those wigs were taking up too much space in my life, physically and emotionally. I'd gotten caught up in trying to be what other people wanted me to be and not being my true authentic self. So I chopped off all of my hair. No half measures for me! I went natural and discovered I really loved my fro. I binged on YouTube videos until I learned to care for my natural hair in all its glory. The fastest way to lasting transformation is to love yourself as you are.

A few years passed, and I'm loving my hair. It was long and beautiful, and I was so proud of it. At a business meeting, a colleague asked if he could send my photo to *Oxygen*. It had been a while since I'd tried to book it, and I wasn't in the shape I'd been in before, but I thought, *Why not?* A week later, I heard back: "We would love to have you." I hit the roof. I was so excited. Then I burst into tears. I knew it was about the hair. Until I loved myself and owned my beauty, no one else would. Booking that cover meant so much to me because it affirmed the power of self-love and authenticity.

At the shoot, I felt good, fit and rockin' my natural hair. Then a stylist asked, "Is that the top you're going to wear?" I guessed she was really talking about my boobs. I started freaking out. I hadn't brought any silicone cutlets to pump the girls up. Desperate, I raced to the bathroom and stuffed my bra with the only thing I had: sports socks. I smoothed and tucked, but no matter what I did, I looked lumpy—and ridiculous. My comical image in the mirror snapped me to my senses. Tossing those balled-up socks on the floor, I called myself out: *Koya, stop it. You're beautiful. Walk back out there. Get in front of the camera. Be beautiful.* And I did. I went out there strong and confident and did some of my best modeling work ever. That cover image makes me proud because it reminds me how important it is to challenge each and every one of the limiting beliefs that prevent me from appreciating my natural beauty—hair, boobs, brains, and all.

Challenging your limiting beliefs is humbling work. You think you've got one beat, and then another one crops up. You're feeling strong, and then you have a moment when you lose your self-confidence again. It's okay. It happens. The following practices will help you work through those moments, and eventually, it'll get easier. You'll be able to talk yourself through your limiting beliefs like I did in that bathroom. The work is worth it. Being 100 percent comfortable with yourself and living 100 percent from your authentic self is the only way to move from fear-based living to love-based living, find your truth, and live it.

You are you, and that's your superpower.

yoga practice: camel pose

- Begin kneeling with your knees hip-width apart.
- Come onto your toes.
- Place your hands on your lower back.
- Lengthen your spine and expand your chest with an inhale.
- Slowly arch your back with an exhale, keeping your hips over your knees.
- One at a time, bring your hands to the insides of your ankles.
- Rest your neck in a neutral position.

- Hold the pose and take slow, deep breaths.
- Return your hands to your back; then rise with an inhale and sit back on your heels.
- Modification: Keep your hands on your lower back to lessen the stretch.
- Hold pose for 3 to 5 breaths and relax in Child's Pose.
- Repeat three times.

FROM LIMITING TO LIBERATING

Limiting beliefs can be transformed from beliefs that prevent you from connecting with your authentic self to ones that deepen your connection to it. What you do is this:

1. Identify them.

2. Challenge them.

3. Switch them to a positive.

4. Learn from them.

Identifying Limiting Beliefs

What are the limiting beliefs that are holding you back? What are the negative beliefs about who you are or how you imagine other people see you that prevent you from doing what you most want to do? Limiting beliefs often include words such as "enough," "always," "never," "everyone," and "no one." For example:

I'm not smart enough.
I'm always ridiculed.
I never have enough support.
I can't do it because everyone wants to see me fail.
I won't succeed because no one understands me.

Self-judgment can help us become the best we can be, or it can hold us back. Reflecting on your actions and asking *How can I do that better?* is a good thing. Looking at yourself and saying *I'm stupid* or *I'm not worthy* is not.

In middle school, I tried out for the cheerleading team and didn't make it. It was the first time I'd ever tried out for anything. I hadn't cheered before or gone to cheerleading camp like some of the other girls, but I thought, *I'm athletic; I can do this.* I was so nervous, I could barely catch my breath. But I made it through my routine and felt good about it.

When I didn't make the team, I felt, *I'm not good enough.* I'd *never* felt that way before. But it didn't shut me down. It made me want to practice and train harder. I couldn't audition for cheerleading again until the next year, but track team tryouts were soon. I went out for the team and made it. I may not have been good enough at cheering, but I was good enough at track—and lots of other things. When you focus only on what you perceive as your weaknesses, self-judgment becomes harmful. And when negative self-judgment becomes a pattern, it turns into a limiting belief.

You may not realize a limiting belief is at work in your life. These beliefs can become so ingrained that we aren't able to recognize them until we dig a little deeper.

What areas of your life do you frequently complain about? Do you feel regularly frustrated by a part of your life? Complaints and frustrations are often signs of a limiting belief. In this way, they're good things, telling you to look closer at what you're doing because it isn't aligning with what you *should* be doing. They're pushing you to be truer to who you are and to be a better version of yourself.

So what frustrates you? Is there a limiting belief buried beneath that frustration? Hint: limiting beliefs can sound a lot like excuses. For example:

I hate my job.

Limiting belief: I'm not smart enough to get a different job.

My partner doesn't respect me.

Limiting belief: I don't deserve a good relationship.

I wish there wasn't so much trash on my block.

Limiting belief: I don't know the right people to tackle this problem.

As a perfectionist, I have to be careful not to let the limiting belief "I'm not ready" hold me back from getting things done. I want everything to be perfect: my website, my teaching materials, my videos, *everything.* I hold myself to a high standard— so high that it could have meant I never took the leap to share my projects with the world because I don't think they are ever good enough.

I'm good at having "reasons" why I'm not ready yet—it's not the right time; I still have more to do—but they are really just the excuses of a perfectionist. The truth is I'm procrastinating. Take this book, for example. I could have written a book five years ago, but I thought, *It needs be perfect and include everything I've learned about mental, spiritual, and physical health in the last decade.* Overwhelmed, I put the idea of writing a book aside: *I'm not ready,* I told myself. But then I grew frustrated that I hadn't written a book and wasn't able to share my ideas in that way. Once I acknowledged this frustration and identified the limiting belief behind it, I could challenge it.

Perfectionism and procrastination can prevent you from pursuing your passions.

Common limiting beliefs:

I'm not good enough.

I'm not strong enough.

I don't have enough support.

I don't have enough resources.

I don't have the skills.

I don't have enough money.

I live in the wrong part of the world.

I have to wait until I lose weight.

I'm too old.

I'm too young.

I don't have enough time.

Write out three beliefs that are holding you back. List them here, keeping in mind that as you write them down, they are losing power over you. You are creating space between you and these limiting beliefs. Eventually we will cut those limiting beliefs from your life altogether. Write down all that apply to you, and feel how you are detoxing them out of your system as you write them out. On the next full moon, a time of tremendous energy, burn them and flush them down the toilet.

Three of my limiting beliefs are:

1. _____

2. _____

3. _____

Challenging Limiting Beliefs

Once you've identified a limiting belief, consider: Is it true? For example:

<u>Limiting belief: I'm not ready to write a book.</u>

Question: Is it true that I'm not ready to write a book?
Answer: No. I'm ready to write a book. I don't have to write the perfect book; I can write a good book that reflects my unique point of view. I am ready to do my best.

<u>Limiting belief: I'm not good enough.</u>

Question: Is it true that I'm not good enough?
Answer: No. I'm good enough to do my best.

<u>Limiting belief: I'm not strong enough.</u>

Question: Is it true that I'm not strong enough?
Answer: No. I'm strong enough to do my best.

<u>Limiting belief: I don't have enough support.</u>

Question: Is it true that I don't have enough support?
Answer: No. I do feel supported by others.

It may be true that you don't feel you have enough support in one particular area of your life. Maybe you don't feel as if you have backing from your family to go back to school or change jobs or start eating better. But is absolutely every family member dismissing you? Is there a friend who is supportive? A co-worker? An online community? Instead of thinking of the negative, think of the positive. Instead of thinking of all of the people who tear you down, think about the people who love you. Find the positive and attract more support into your life.

Masterpieces aren't built overnight, and you *are a masterpiece.*

There is only one you, and you can do things as beautifully as you can do them. And that is enough. Make a commitment to do your best, and watch a lot of limiting beliefs lose their power over you. When you do your best, it doesn't matter if the end result is perfect. Doing your best is like spreading seeds on the ground. Some seeds are going to fall on fertile earth and blossom into flowers. Your seeds may not yield exactly what you wanted (or thought you wanted), but they will sprout something beautiful.

It's easier to do your best when you stop comparing yourself to others or trying to be better than someone else. Move out of a competitive and comparative mind-set. It only fosters resentment for others and feelings of inadequacy. Focus on being your best self, and have compassion and self-love for wherever you are in your journey. Allow others to inspire you instead of intimidating you. You don't need to be like anyone else or do the things they do. Find your authentic self and what works for you. Love yourself first and most.

When I challenged my own limiting belief, I asked, *Is it true that my voice isn't good enough?*

My answer: *No. My voice is good enough to share; it's beautiful, and I want to share it with the world.*

I didn't recognize that for a while because I had accepted someone else's judgment. I know now that I am responsible for my emotions—even if they are triggered by another person. I could have taken what my dad said differently, as an uncharacteristic moment of irritation rather than a judgment on whether I should sing at all. Instead, based on what happened to me as a young girl, I created the limiting beliefs that "I'm not good enough" and "no one wants to hear me sing." And these aren't the truth. Since I created those limiting beliefs, I have the power to destroy them and cleanse them from my system. And so do you.

Challenge your limiting beliefs. Are they true?

Limiting belief: _____

Consider: Is it true?

My answer: _____

_____

Limiting belief: _____

Consider: Is it true?

My answer: _____

_____

Limiting belief: _____

Consider: Is it true?

My answer: _____

_____

"I don't have enough money"

I hear this limiting belief a lot. I don't have enough money to go there, to get an education, to have a personal trainer. People give money so much power. To me, money is energy. When you say you don't have enough money, you're basically saying you don't have enough energy. Try looking at money as energy, and see if it's easier find more of it.

Switch a Limiting Belief to a Positive

Stop a limiting belief in its tracks by acknowledging that it's something you're working on. In this way you immediately re-invent it as a positive change you are making. You may have the limiting belief "I am always late." Rephrase it as "I am working on being on time." You can use this with any limiting belief:

- I am working on being ready to write my book.
- I am working on making my voice the best that it can be.

I realized recently that I have a limiting belief about why I'd been unable to find the ideal partner: I'll never find a guy who loves me for being vegan, spiritual, and driven. Is it true? No! But I'd been holding myself back from dating because of this negative thought in my head. And my negative energy attracted more of the same. No wonder I would submit my requirements on a bunch of dating apps and get zero possibilities. It took a hard sit-down for me to look this limiting belief in the face and switch it up. I now could say, "I am working on finding a guy who loves me for being vegan, spiritual, and driven." I got myself back out there, started dating again, and met an amazing man who appreciates and loves every part of me, the man of my dreams. It never would have happened if I were still carrying around that limiting belief.

If you keep playing a negative story in your mind, you'll find it hard to get what you want. Challenge your limiting beliefs to find a positive story.

From Petty to Positive

Switch your limiting beliefs to a positive, empowering affirmation:

Limiting belief: _____

Positive affirmation: I'm working on _____

_____

Limiting belief: _____

Positive affirmation: I'm working on _____

_____

Limiting belief: _____

Positive affirmation: I'm working on _____

_____

Learn from a Limiting Belief

Your limiting beliefs are telling you where you need help. What is your limiting belief telling you that you need to cultivate? Who or what do you need to invite into your life to help you move beyond your limiting belief?

- To bring more confidence about my voice into my life, I've started working with a voice coach.

- To help me be ready and not sit on a project until it's "perfect," I team up with other people who can help me follow through. If a friend or colleague says, "Let's just do it; let's get it out," then I'll do it. That extra push is all I need to stop the procrastination and excuses.

- To help me find a partner who aligns with my lifestyle, I've invited more openness and flexibility into my life.

Learning from a limiting belief means asking for help. Owning your limiting belief is the first step, but if you're just owning it and not getting the help you need to move beyond it, then you're procrastinating. You can keep making excuses—it's not my time; I'm thinking about it; I'll wait on a sign—but the truth is, you make the right time, and signs are great, but you have to do the work. Why not start right now?

You have the answers inside of you. Ask for help, find the resources you need, and let the grandest version of you express itself. Learn from your limiting beliefs. What do you need to cultivate? Who do you need to invite into your life to help you move beyond your limiting beliefs? Write down three things you can learn:

1. _____

2. _____

3. _____

Here's what transforming my limiting beliefs looks like:

Identify	Challenge	Switch	Learn
My voice isn't good enough.	My voice is beautiful.	I'm working on making my voice stronger.	I'm practicing with a voice coach.
I'm not ready to express myself in a book.	I am ready to do my best.	I'm gaining skills every day to become more ready.	I'm hiring a talented team to help me accomplish my goal.
I'll never find a partner who aligns with my lifestyle.	I will find the right partner for me.	I'm actively meeting new people.	I'm opening myself up to connecting with diverse people.

meditation practice

Follow the numbered meditation instructions on pages 14–15 and use the following as your intention:

I am worthy of love, acceptance, and peace of mind. I am worthy of the best things in life. I deserve to be happy and loved. I abundantly manifest everything in alignment with the life I want to live.

THE BEST VERSION OF YOU

Challenging and transforming your limiting beliefs gets you closer to your authentic self—who you are without your limiting beliefs. We're so willing to repeat what we see as the bad about ourselves but not the good. It's time to break that habit. Who are you without your limiting beliefs? Concentrate on your gifts, talents, and positive qualities. Make a list of ten of your positive qualities, gifts, and talents:

1. _____

2. _____

3. _____

4. _____

5. _____

6. _____

7. _____

8. _____

9. _____

10. _____

Writing down your positive qualities is a powerful way of affirming them. It's important to be aware of this list every day. Stick it on your closet door or in another place where you'll see it regularly, and each time you notice it, remind yourself what you're good at. Doing so will fill you with confidence, and you'll be deeply rooted in that confidence throughout the day. Notice that when you focus on this list every day, you remain in a place of peace, power, and love no matter who or what tries to sway you.

Remember: No Judgment

Limiting beliefs are fear. What if for one day you didn't live in fear? What if for one day you didn't judge yourself, others, or the world? What if you accepted it all and your part in it just like you accept day and night—and repeated this attitude daily?

affirmation practice

Say this affirmation several times upon waking in the morning and before going to bed at night:

I release negative thoughts about myself, others, and the world.

CHAPTER FIVE

You're Too Blessed to Be Stressed

It's easy to get caught up in the negative and focus on all of the things we lack or that cause us stress. But complaining and criticizing yourself and other people is a way of living in fear, one that lowers your vibration, attracting more negativity. Living from a place of gratitude by thinking about the ways you're blessed raises your vibration. When you are able to acknowledge how grateful you are for something in your life—and hopefully there are many people and things you could be grateful for, such as your health or your friends—instead of focusing on the sister who betrayed you or the former boss who let you go, you're living in gratitude. In times when we're experiencing a lot of negatives, it's especially important to look at this list of blessings. It will help you to realize that even in the darkest times, we're too blessed to be stressed.

Every day when I pray, my prayers are of gratitude. God and the universe already know what I need, and so asking for something just isn't necessary. Instead, I express my gratitude to God and the universe for giving me everything that I need. Every day, I acknowledge that I already *have* everything that I need in my mind. Doing so puts me in the vibration of *attracting* everything that I need emotionally and physically.

GRATITUDE GETS YOU BY

Ever since I was a little girl, gratitude has been a really important part of my life. My family and our church taught me to be thankful for all that we had, even if we didn't have very much. Now I express gratitude every day and feel the power it has in my life.

But it was really hard to be grateful when my grandma passed. She'd been a second mom to me, and I wasn't ready for her to go. People live a long time in my family. I'd thought we would have more time together and she'd be here until she was 109, or at least 103. When she passed in her 80s, I was shocked. At first, I was in complete disbelief. She'd been sick, but I'd thought, *She'll get better.* When she died, I felt sad, hurt, and robbed. I was angry that she left too soon and angry at the universe for taking her from me. I was afraid no one would ever love me again like my grandma had loved me. I felt guilty for not going to see her in the hospital because I thought she'd get well. I felt a lot of emotions that weren't love or gratitude. I was in a place of deep sadness, caught in a low vibration.

Then an intuitive coach asked me, "What are the things you love about your grandma?" My list went on and on with all of the times we had spent together. My grandma showed me how to be loving and nurturing, how to care for others, cook, dress, keep a clean home, and pay attention to detail. Her impact on me was huge. There isn't a corner of my life that she didn't touch.

Making that list helped me to focus on all of the ways my grandma blessed my life by taking care of me. Until I expressed gratitude for her life and our time together, I couldn't leave that place of sadness, and I wasn't able to see that her soul and her spirit are still here with me. Once I elevated my mind-set to that of gratitude, I could experience her love as present with me every day. I still miss her so much, but I am grateful for the beautiful blessing she was in my life. Her love will be with me forever, and in that way, she's always here, not gone.

Physical distance separates me from my parents, brothers, sisters, nieces, and nephews. I feel I was led to move to California, but leaving my family behind in Tennessee was tough, and I miss them all very much, especially the children. Sometimes, I get so sad that I'm not there to see my nieces and nephews growing up, to play with them or see and touch them every day. When the loneliness becomes overwhelming, I know it's time to look around me and appreciate the family I have worldwide. My "play parents" on the West Coast love and care for me as if I were their own child. I remind myself of the smiling faces of the school kids in California to whom I am blessed to teach yoga. I may not be surrounded by my blood family, but I can spend time with people who love me. Appreciating them and spending more time with them immediately makes me feel better.

When times are tough, it's gratitude for what you have that will help get you by.

The Power of Gratitude

If you've experienced a loss and can't seem to move out of sadness, make a list of all of the ways your loved one was a blessing in your life. What are you grateful for? Look at this list every morning until you start to feel better.

I am grateful for_____

_____

_____

_____

_____

Then look around you. Where do you see the love, nurturing, or other qualities that you experienced from your loved one? Where are those qualities still available to you? Write down a few, and be grateful for what you still have at this moment.

I see the love in _____

_____

_____

_____

Choose Gratitude; Choose Love

Expressing gratitude, and really *feeling* grateful for something, completely shifts your energy and opens you up to receive even more to be thankful for. When you're in a state of gratitude, you're better able to attract more of what you want in life. You are in the vibration of love, and everything that's in alignment with that vibration is in your life. When you're in the vibration of fear, judgment, or sadness, you're in a lower vibration. It's okay to be there; you just don't want to stay there, as you'll attract more of the same. The frequency of sadness will attract more and more sadness. Here's what's important: you have the power to choose your vibration. Choose the vibration of love and gratitude.

Let's say you're sad, like I was when my grandma passed. Once you choose gratitude and start thinking about your blessings, you'll raise your vibrations and come out of that sadness. You're back in the vibration of love.

Choosing gratitude is not to say you will never experience sadness. It's choosing to switch your vibration from one of sadness to one of gratitude. It's choosing to switch from fear-based living to love-based living. Gratitude and love are choices you can always make. There is always something to be grateful for.

Life can be beautiful and a beautiful mess all at the same time. When the mess is hitting you hard, stop the dial on love and focus on your blessings.

yoga practice:
wide leg forward fold

- Stand with your feet together.
- Step your feet 3 to 5 feet apart.
- Bring feet parallel to each other.
- Place your hands on your hips.
- Lengthen your spine with an inhale.
- Bend forward with an exhale, keeping your spine long.

- Bring your fingertips or palms to the floor, and walk them back until they're in line with your feet.

- Relax your neck, and draw your shoulders away from your ears.

- Hold the pose and take slow, deep breaths.

- Bring your hands to your hips, bend your knees, and engage your back muscles.

- Inhale, and slowly rise with a flat back.

- Exhale to step your feet together.

- Modification: Bend knees slightly throughout.

- Hold for 5 to 10 breaths; repeat three times with 30 seconds' rest.

ALWAYS ELEVATE

I encounter so many people, especially on social media, who think being authentic is about showing and sharing how sad they are and how many negative things are happening in their lives. Sharing is okay if it helps you to move from a low vibration to a higher one, but lots of people are staying in that low vibration for a long time because they think, *This is how I'm being relatable; this is how I'm being vulnerable.* But then they wonder, *Why am I still so sad?* I know why: chances are they've lost themselves in a vibration of sadness and disappointment!

People wonder why I don't need a detox from social media. They ask me how I can post, and post, and post, and not get burned out. It's because I share when I'm going through things—bad days, struggles, and dark times—but I also share *how I get through things.* I don't stay in that lower vibration of anger and sadness all of the time. If I stay there, I will burn out. That place brings you down. It's exhausting—very exhausting. And if I stay in a lower vibration, how am I going to help others? It's impossible. I know I have to keep myself from staying immersed in negative emotions all of the time. Choosing gratitude is how I elevate.

Think of it this way: if 50 percent of your time is spent in sadness, you need to make a shift. You're in danger of getting stressed out. Your health is going to start to suffer. Spending even half of your time in this lower vibration of sadness will take your health away from you.

Life is not about being hurt or feeling sad. A lot of people think they need to suffer in order to grow, that the universe wants them to go through a season of mourning. I don't believe that. You can mourn if that's what you need to do, but it's not necessary to stay there.

The only way to get through the hard times is to think about your blessings, to think about the things you're grateful for, and to get yourself into a frequency of love as soon as you can. Try to feel happy 70 to 90 percent of the time. If you can do this, you're generally going to feel good. You'll feel sadness and other negative emotions, but you will not dwell in them. You'll be dwelling in gratitude.

> *Fear encourages more fear, and love encourages more love. I choose love.*

KNOW YOUR A-TEAM

Who do you turn to when you feel at your lowest? Who do you trust? With whom do you share your innermost thoughts, feelings, and worries knowing that they have your best interests at heart and do not judge you? It is important to surround yourself with positive and inspiring people, but it's more important to have close, meaningful relationships.

You can have a ton of upbeat acquaintances, but if you don't have a true friend, you're going to have a tough time when something goes wrong. Having an A-Team of people who have your back when you need support and who stand by your side when you are feeling down, reminding you of your strengths and celebrating your victories, is one of the most precious things in the world.

So who's on your A-Team? I suggest including a mentor, someone who inspires you by sharing their life journey. Try to talk to your mentor at least once a month, weekly if possible, and the other members of your team every day if possible. Share your hopes and desires but also your frustrations. This A-Team will get you through your toughest times and help you stay on track with your goals. Show gratitude for the members of your A-Team regularly. Tell them how much you value having them in your life.

Feel as if you don't have an A-Team? Don't worry! Now is the perfect time to consider how to deepen the friendships you currently have or to widen your circle. Close relationships rely on open, thoughtful, honest conversation. Do you need to dedicate some time to a friend in order to reconnect and catch up? Today, it's so easy to meet new people. Open yourself up to meeting others, in real life or through social media. Start with folks who share one of your strong interests. I have expanded my A-Team through the valuable connections I've made through the yoga community on Instagram. Even a few friends make all the difference. List your top three below:

My A-Team:

Team Member 1: _____

_____

Team Member 2: _____

_____

Team Member 3: _____

_____

TAKE ACTION

If you're struggling to switch over to gratitude, consider: Is there something you could do about what's making you sad? How can you take this action? I was becoming increasingly sad and frustrated over the lack of inclusivity in the yoga world and how the "Spirit" was being left out of most yoga practices. *Well,* I thought, *what are you going to do about it? Are you going to just complain about it every day?* I decided to act and created a yoga teacher training to educate, inspire, and certify as many women of color as possible in all eight limbs of yoga. Starting the Get Loved Up Yoga School has been one of the most challenging and rewarding things I've ever done. It's made me grateful for the transformation and healing I've seen happen before my eyes and the blessings I know these teachers will share with the world.

Taking action puts you in a frequency of gratitude. And once you are in gratitude, everything in that frequency comes to your aid. Every person in that frequency comes to partner with you to bring your dream alive.

meditation practice

Follow the numbered meditation instructions on pages 14–15 and use the following as your intention:

I release negative thoughts about myself, others, and the world. I am enough as I am now, and every day I make time for self-care and expressing my creativity.

EXPRESS GRATITUDE EVERY DAY

I practice gratitude every single day through prayer. Prayer is how I express my appreciation for all the blessings in my life. It's my way of saying thank you. Prayer isn't the only way, though. Make a gratitude list each morning, keep a gratitude journal, or find another way that feels right to you. But do it consistently, each and every day. Often, we spend our entire day talking about the chaos around us. A daily gratitude practice brings our attention back to what's really important—how much we've been blessed.

Gratitude Journal and Gratitude Prayer

Two of my favorite ways to practice gratitude are to keep a gratitude journal and say a gratitude prayer each morning. Use a notebook or your phone as a gratitude journal, and record the three things you are grateful for each day. Struggling to come up with three? Think extra hard. Did you overcome any challenges today? Is there something to be grateful for in that experience?

I begin my gratitude prayer by saying "I am grateful for," and then I list at least three things I'm grateful for and why.

Practice gratitude consistently. Trust me. It's pretty magical.

Be a Blessing

Acts of kindness put you in a vibration of gratitude. As long as we're still living, we can be a blessing to someone. And when we're a blessing to someone, we're living in love. When was the last time you told a friend how much they mean to you? Or sent a thank-you card? Or did a random act of kindness, like paying for the person behind you in line at the juice bar? Random acts of kindness are my favorite thing to do. Make them a part of your day. Expressing gratitude will make you, and the people around you, feel better.

Seven-Day Be-a-Blessing Challenge

Do a random act of kindness each day for seven days. Record what you did and how it made you feel in your gratitude journal.

Remember: Run the Race in the Sun

Life is a race. You can run it in shoes that fit well and in good weather. Or you can run it in ill-fitting, nasty shoes through mud and rain. It's your choice. Choosing gratitude is choosing a nice pair of shoes to run in. Choosing gratitude is choosing to run in the sun.

PART II

Live Your Truth

affirmation practice

Say this affirmation several times upon waking in the morning and before going to bed at night:

I trust my soul's guidance and go within to work things out.

CHAPTER SIX

Knowledge Is Power

I'm forever a teacher, but I'm always a student. Opening myself up to knowledge in all of its forms has given me the self-esteem and confidence to identify my ideal life and pursue it with passion. Constantly learning new things about myself and the world and allowing myself to connect with others has opened doors for me in every area of my life—my career, my health, my relationships, and my spirituality—in ways I never could have planned or imagined. Self-knowledge, knowing who I am and what I want, gives me the strength and positive energy to pursue my goals with passion and determination. It can do the same for you.

You've already learned so much about yourself. You know your fears and the limiting beliefs that create them. You have the tools to challenge them and the self-love practices so you can breathe into them and release them. You know how to live as a creator, empowered and in charge of your future. You're using gratitude to raise your vibration. This is just the beginning. Now you're ready to reconnect with your authentic self and learn what drives and inspires you and what your ideal life looks like. Once you know that, you can start making it a reality. Self-knowledge is essential, but so is learning about this great big beautiful universe that we live in and all of the people sharing it with us.

Recently, I was blown away by the sights, sounds, and culture of Morocco. Walking through the dusty alleyways of the medina, crammed with stalls piled high with clothing, jewelry, pottery, and spices and bursting with the voices of haggling vendors, I was far, far away from the quiet beaches of California. I'd never imagined going to Morocco, but the moment I saw my friend's eye-popping pictures of her visit to Marrakesh, I put it high on my list. It called to me in such a powerful way. Immediately, I knew in my heart it was time for me to get out of my bubble of familiarity and experience a radically different place. And that I should do it alone. I know, right?! Alone in Morocco? For me, it couldn't get more challenging than that. Sure, I've traveled internationally before, but never to somewhere so culturally different from my own experience, and never alone. I've always been part of a group or retreat, often as a teacher or coach and always around others and holding space for them. This time, I wanted to hold space for me. It had been a chaotic and emotionally draining few months. I was still reeling from my auntie's illness and the physical and emotional pain caused by a recent sexual assault. I needed time and space to heal. Morocco would be the answer.

I won't lie; I had concerns. I worried about how I might be treated as a woman and as a minority traveling solo. I took steps to feel comfortable and safe, including hiring a highly recommended private driver to accompany me every day. And then I decided to live each moment in Morocco fiercely. I'd embrace everything the landscape, people, food, and culture had to offer and trust my judgment and intuition to make good decisions. The beautiful thing about travel is how it challenges you. You never know what you'll do in a totally new situation, especially one that puts you way outside of your comfort zone. But you never know if you stay in your bubble. It's harder to learn when you're closed off from new experiences.

I learned right away that I could very easily be taken advantage of in the medina, the atmospheric old part of the city, with labyrinthine alleyways and market stalls. Children would ask for money, and I'd give it to them. A vendor would raise the price of an item I wanted to purchase, and I would pay whatever they asked, no matter how outrageous. I couldn't haggle to save my life! It's not that surprising, really. I know I'm a natural giver. If someone asks me for something and I have it, and it doesn't hurt me to give it, I'll give it. You can see the problem with this in Morocco, though: in five minutes, I'd be broke and left with nothing if I kept giving everything away. I had to check in with myself: *Koya, you cannot be how you normally are because you're gonna get taken advantage of. Period. That's just the reality of it. You have to decide what that means to you.*

For me, this meant only visiting the medina during the day, when the crowds were thinner and the frenzy was less intense. I knew myself enough to understand that I wouldn't do well in the chaos of the medina at night. So I stayed away. I enjoyed the light haggling common during the day, set better personal space boundaries, and asked my driver for help if a situation started to feel overwhelming or unsafe. I acknowledged my authentic, giving self and made choices that remained true to it without being taken advantage of or worse. This trip pushed me out of my comfort zone and tested my limits. It felt so empowering. I knew myself enough to know what was right for me, and I was okay living that truth.

Knowing who I am and what I want gives me the strength and positive energy to pursue my goals with passion and determination. Knowing I have the skills, tools, and team to make my dreams a reality fires me up and pushes me forward, no matter what might get in my way. By looking inward and outside of myself, I gain valuable knowledge and the self-assurance that comes with it.

The fear that holds so many us back is self-doubt. We're not sure what we want in life and don't trust our hearts when they speak to us. We doubt our ability to change or try new things or handle new experiences. We wonder if we have the education, skills, or resources to achieve our goals.

Knowledge is the answer to those doubts. Knowledge is the launchpad for everything you want to be or do in life. Knowledge is power.

GET UNSTUCK

When I say "knowledge is power," a lot of people think, *Yeah, I went to college, and that's good enough for me.* That's not it at all. The knowledge I'm talking about is not tied to a specific degree or accreditation. It's not *tied* to anything. It's not static. It has no end point. The knowledge I mean is dynamic, constantly growing, shifting, and changing—because the world and everything in it is constantly changing. When we commit to gaining this type of knowledge, we commit to an awareness of all the universe has to teach us, in every moment and in every experience. We are mindful—eager even—to learn new things about ourselves and the people, places, and things that surround us.

Without this awareness, we get stuck, lost in the darkness of the past instead of living in the present and preparing appropriately for the future. Seeking new knowledge, especially by connecting with new people, can be scary. It makes us vulnerable and opens us up to the risk of being hurt. The risk is worth it. The rewards are worth it. Staying safe, staying small, is much riskier.

The world is always changing. Seek new knowledge in any way you can, and keep changing with it. It doesn't have to mean traveling halfway around the world (though I recommend it!). There are opportunities to unstick yourself in practically every moment of each day if you keep your eyes open. Walk a different way to school, click on that new podcast, introduce yourself to a new co-worker, try that yoga class, ask questions—about anything. Embrace your curiosity. I've embraced mine by being constantly open to travel, connecting with new people, and exploring spiritual teachings, and it has brought so much knowledge, change, and compassion into my life. What might it bring to yours?

yoga practice:
bridge pose to wheel pose

- Lie on your back.
- Bend your knees and bring your feet near your buttocks, hip-width apart.
- Rest your arms by your sides, palms down.
- With an inhale, push into your feet to lift your hips.
- Reach your chest toward your chin.
- Clasp your hands underneath you and tuck your shoulders under.
- Hold the pose and take slow, deep breaths.
- Unclasp your hands, then exhale to lower.

Modification: Keep arms flat on the floor to lessen the stretch in the shoulders.

- Lie on your back with your feet flat on the floor, knees bent.

- Bring your feet hip-width apart.

- Reach your arms up with an inhale.

- Place your palms next to your head, fingers pointing toward your shoulders.

- Keep your forearms parallel.

- Press your hands and feet into the floor with an exhale, and very gently come to the top of your head.

- Pause.

- Straighten your arms and legs on your next inhalation.

- Press your chest forward.

- Let your head hang.

- Hold the pose and breathe normally.

- Carefully lower your head and then whole body to the floor with an exhale.

Modification: Come to the top of your head only and stay here for one breath.

KNOW THYSELF

Self-knowledge is the most important kind of knowledge you can have and the foundation for living fierce. How can you make your dreams come true if you don't know what they are? How can you create your ideal life when you don't know what that looks like to you?

Self-knowledge can be scary. It requires you to look inward, and sometimes there are things about ourselves that we'd rather not know or are afraid to confront. Or we're afraid of what other people might think of us or say about us if we start living in alignment with our hearts—especially if that means changing. How many times have you made a positive change in your life to find a family member or your significant other telling you, "You're not being yourself"? Or even "You're not being authentic"? If you want to change, even though it may make you uncomfortable at times, self-knowledge will show you the path to follow and give you the confidence to stay on it no matter what others say. Getting to know who you are may even pleasantly surprise you. In fact, I know it will.

You leave your body; you take your soul. Connect to it.

I started singing again because I truly love performing and sharing my voice with others. I expected to enjoy recording my first song, but I didn't expect to discover that I have a talent for production. Producing my music video sparked a creative impulse in me I didn't know I had. I'd never produced a video before, but I didn't overthink it. I didn't let my fear or nervousness get in the way; I just started doing it, hiring a co-writer, talent, and videographer. Everything came together easily and effortlessly. And when I reflected on why, I recognized how well I was able to express my vision for the video and communicate with the team—and how gratified I felt doing it. I thought, *I'm really good at this, and I really love it!*

Now I want to produce more projects. Who knows where this desire will take me? I didn't know where yoga would take me either, but I have faith that I should follow where my passion leads me.

Know Thyself

Can you believe that someone asked me to name my favorite musician, and I couldn't do it? You'd be amazed at how much about yourself you don't know or haven't thought about in a while. Take the time now to reflect and reconnect with your authentic self. Write your answers here or in your gratitude journal.

Health

What is your blood type? _____

Do you have any allergies? _____

Do you have any chronic pain or injuries? _____

Likes and Interests

What is your favorite:

Color? _____

Hobby? _____

Book? _____

Band? _____

Vacation spot? _____

What makes you smile? _____

If you could choose to do anything for a day, what would it be?

_____

Values
What are three of your core values?

1. _____

2. _____

3. _____

What motivates you to work hard? _____

_____

What is your proudest accomplishment? _____

_____

What are three adjectives you would use to describe yourself?

1. _____

2. _____

3. _____

Who, or what, was your biggest teacher? _____

_____

What's the best piece of advice you've ever been given?

_____

Goals

What are your career-related goals? _____

_____

What would you change about yourself if you could?

_____

Where do you see yourself in 10 years?

_____

If you could master one skill, what would it be? Why?

_____

Morning Pages

Morning is my favorite time to get my heart out. First thing, before you even get out of bed, write down what you feel. Don't overthink it. Just do a stream-of-consciousness, in-the-moment brain dump. I do this every morning as a way of checking in with myself and making sure my feelings and actions are in alignment. If I notice that I'm filling my morning pages with negative emotions such as sadness, stress, or frustration, I know I'm not in alignment and I need make a change somewhere in my life.

HONOR YOUR "NO" AND YOUR "NOT RIGHT NOW"

Self-knowledge isn't just about knowing what you want. It's also about knowing what you don't want. When your intuition tells you no, you need to listen to that no. In Morocco, when I chose not to go to the medina at night, I heard a no and respected it. A few people tried to change my mind. "Oh, you have to do that!

You can't leave Morocco without going to the medina at night. Isn't that why you came to Morocco in the first place? Don't be a coward. Don't you want to be fearless?" Not that kind of fearless! Not the kind of fearless that ignores my inner truth. Doing that isn't being fearless at all. It's being foolish and disrespectful to your authentic self.

> *Being fierce is about constantly pushing your boundaries—and discovering where they are.*

KNOW WHAT YOU DON'T KNOW

Self-knowledge can bring the realization of what you don't know—the things that you need to learn to help you achieve your ideal reality. This realization is just as important as—if not more important than—knowing what you *do* know. When you identify what you need to learn in order to move forward, you can make a plan and take steps to acquire that information or skill. Don't let what you don't know be a roadblock! Let it open up new doors like it did for me on my journey to become a yoga and meditation teacher and holistic health coach.

It's scary making a commitment to get more knowledge. Who knows what you might discover or where it might take you? The unknown is always a little frightening. But you are strong enough to challenge those fears and flexible enough to adapt to change. The new knowledge and tools you gain on your journey will bless your life.

Tips for Being a Good Listener

Listening is an essential skill if you want to communicate well with others and learn from them. To be a good listener, you need to practice these behaviors:

- Be warm and attentive.

- Show that you are listening. Nod or make affirming noises.

- Show that you are paying attention and trying to understand. Ask for clarifications, details, or explanations.

- Let what the speaker has said sink in before responding. Don't give a snap reply or make a quick judgment.

- Allow silence. Don't immediately fill a pause. Allow the talker to share in their own way. If you feel a silence is becoming awkward, ask a gentle question.

ATTITUDE MATTERS

Attitude is so important when it comes to learning. With a positive attitude, you'll learn. You may need a tutor or teacher to help you, and it may take a while for you to gain understanding and mastery, but you will learn. A negative attitude prevents you from being open-minded enough to learn. You won't even *hear* what's being taught.

I struggled to keep a positive attitude when I was transitioning to a plant-based diet. I knew I wanted to be healthier and understood the positive impact that eating this way would have on the planet . . . but I could not figure out how to make it work for me. I'd get discouraged, and as if on cue there would be a chorus of people telling me how it definitely didn't work for them, either. They'd tried it and weren't successful, so the implication was, why should I keep trying? Their negative energy brought my vibration down. But I was determined and open to learning as much as I could about the various options and approaches out there. I had faith that I'd figure out a way to make it work for me eventually. And I did.

Most of those naysayers hadn't done much research on the different ways to eat a plant-based diet. They'd tried it one way, and when it didn't work, that was that. They'd closed themselves off from learning anything new about it—and missed out on what could have been a positive lifestyle change.

Never say, *Okay, that didn't work.* There's never a definitive end to anything. It isn't a question of whether something is "working" or "not working." The question is, what result did I get from trying that? That information will help you approach any situation in a different way. Stay open, stay positive, and keep learning. You never know when the result you're looking for will happen.

INFORMED DECISION OR FOLLOWING THE HERD?

Change just for the sake of change is not beneficial. Changing how you eat or exercise to follow the latest trend does not serve you. Positive change originates from within, reflecting what aligns with your heart. What if you want to eat healthier and move your body in a different way, and the Paleo Diet or a HIIT workout appeals to you?

Do your homework!

Celebrity testimonials and Instagram photos (remember, those can be faked!) do not count. Read up on the practice you're interested in exploring. Are there studies from impartial, reputable sources to support the benefits? Do your research, talk to a certified professional, and get the facts before you dive in.

Ask, *How can this eating or exercise plan work* for me? Your body is unique. With this eating approach, are you getting the nutrients you need? Is it realistic and sustainable given your lifestyle? Look at every aspect of a trend before hopping on board. This takes some time and a little work, but you're worth it. Change based on knowledge, not the most recent trend, will be more likely to last.

THAT LUMP IN YOUR THROAT

Self-knowledge includes knowing when you need help. It's satisfying to do something all on your own, relying only on your talent and drive. But asking for help isn't a sign of failure; it's a sign you are self-aware enough to know what you don't know.

I am always asking for help, but it doesn't come naturally; it's a lesson I'm still learning. I tried to create my first online training course all by myself—write it, star in it, film it, all of it. Everything seemed under control until I tried to upload it. No matter what I did, I couldn't get it to work. I felt like a huge failure. I'd already promised the course to my online community, so I felt that I was letting everyone down. I pride myself on being dependable; I'm a Leo! When I say I'm going to do something, I do it. When the course didn't come out as promised, I was deeply embarrassed and hugely disappointed with myself.

Determined not to give up on the project, I had to take a hard step back and reflect: What could I learn from this situation? The answer: I needed help. I told myself, *You are going to do this right, from start to finish. Stop playing small. You're trying to do everything to create the course and figure out the tech because you're smart, but sometimes you need help from experts.*

Swallowing that lump of disappointment, I started creating the course over again from scratch, beginning with a new assessment:

- How do I put this together?
- What can I do?
- Who do I need to reach out to for the rest?

I identified writing and producing as my strengths. Videography? I'm not the best. I'd hire someone. Being the talent? I'm comfortable in front of the camera, but this video includes a handstand, and I'm not the best at handstands. I'd reach out to people who are. And so on, until I'd hired a team. It took six months to create the course, but it was worth every moment. It came out just as I'd hoped, and I plan on making more.

Once I acknowledged that I could use expert assistance and opened myself up to what others could bring to my project, I found the love in creating the course again. Experts don't have to be only people you hire. Think of your friends, colleagues, neighbors, or online community. When you are open to receiving help, you will find it. Someone, somewhere will help you. As an extra benefit, accomplishing my goal restored my confidence in my ability to follow through. It didn't matter that I didn't do it solo; what matters is that I *did it.*

If you are a new entrepreneur, like me, you may struggle with this. Growing your team is not a failure. It's a sign that you need to expand and let other people do what they're good at to help you reach your goals. When you're trying to build maximum success, you have to let other people in. It took the meltdown of my first attempt at launching an online course for me to accept and gather a team. Now, not only am I proud of the course we created together, I'm also grateful for the individuals I brought on and everything they taught me.

Knowledge is being honest with yourself about what you know and what you don't know—and willing to get help when you need it.

meditation practice

Follow the numbered meditation instructions on pages 14–15 and use the following as your intention:

I trust my soul's guidance and go within to work things out. I have clarity of vision, and my path is revealing itself daily. I allow myself to follow my spontaneous soul urges.

LOVE TOGETHER

There's strength in numbers. You can accomplish great things by yourself, but you can do even more when you are joined by a group of people working with you toward a common goal. We are always sharing our energy with the universe and the people around us, whether we are aware of it or not. When we share our knowledge and love, we share positive energy. When we unite our positive energy with the positive energy of others, beautiful things happen.

I believe in the principle supported by Nelson Mandela: "Each one, teach one." When we teach each other, we elevate the globe. I love sharing what I learn with my community so they can spread those teachings and high vibrations with others. Not only am I a teacher, I am also a student. When I learn, I teach, and when I teach, I learn. We can all learn from one another if we just allow ourselves to listen.

Life is about connecting with our individual souls and the souls around us. One star in the sky doesn't give off much light, but millions of stars shining illuminate the heavens. The more we connect, the brighter that light becomes.

Charity Check

If you have a huge heart like me, you probably like to give to charities that support people in need. It pains me to have to warn you against it, but you can't just support anyone. Yes, there are charities out there that have been accused of extortion, dishonesty, and worse. I've learned the hard way to do research before I support a charity with my money, time, or other resources. Do your homework. Make sure it's a legitimate charity, and review the budget to see how much money actually goes to programming (charitywatch.org is a great resource for this information). Support organizations that elevate the vibration of the universe.

ACCEPT THE TOUGH LESSONS

Sometimes we bring people into our lives because we want to learn from them. We know they have something to share with us or teach us that we need to know. Other times people come into our lives—maybe just for a season—to teach us a lesson that we hadn't expected or anticipated. From them, we may learn about generosity, compassion, and fidelity, gifts we are grateful to receive. Or we may learn difficult, painful truths that cause us distress and heartache. Both types of knowledge enrich our lives because both types make us stronger.

Several years ago a friend whom I trusted stole my identity. I'd opened my home and my heart to this woman, and she ruined my credit and destroyed my trust. How could she do this to me? I couldn't believe it. Afterward, a background check revealed she had a record of embezzlement. The anger from the betrayal filled me. If I'd done that background check sooner, I wouldn't have been so gullible. But who does a background check on a friend? Though I don't do that (regularly), I am now more clear-eyed when it comes to bringing people into my life and personal space. I aim to stay open but not vulnerable to a fault.

My eyes are wide open, but I still miss signs. I remained friends for too long with a woman who consistently showed she wasn't a good friend. She was so focused on herself that she never had room for me. She was a drama queen, and I'm an extreme giver, so I was always trying to help her solve a problem, resolve a crisis, or put out a fire. We'd stay on the phone all night long talking about her issues—and only *her* issues. Even though I did want to share about my life, overall I felt fulfilled because I knew I was being super helpful. It felt good to support and promote her. I wanted love in my life so much that I overlooked the warnings that she wasn't actually a friend to me at all.

A major blowout, sparked by one of her dramas, ended the friendship. I was shocked and hurt by how suddenly it was over. Eventually, we apologized to each other, but we're never, ever going to be friends again. We speak and are cordial, but my hope that she'd be in my life forever, sitting next to me in a rocking chair on a porch when we're both white-haired, is not going to happen. I've had to accept that we're incompatible. Judith Orloff's book *The Empath's Survival Guide* helped me to understand that our dynamic, her playing the role of a narcissist and my playing the role of an empath, was not healthy.

It took me a long time to come to a place of acceptance. I had to talk it out, write it out, and breathe through it for several months before I could let it go. This process made me stronger, and I learned that I can love—but not to the detriment of myself. I find that if I stop loving others when doing so makes me too tired, too exhausted, or too uncomfortable, I grow as a woman and as a leader. I can love, but not if it pushes me beyond my limit of self-care and self-awareness.

Ending these relationships taught me lessons I needed in order to grow and heal.

Too often, we hold on to toxic friendships, family relationships, and romantic partners who hurt us again and again and prevent us from learning the lessons we need to flourish. Ending a relationship is unsettling. But every relationship is not supposed to last forever. Maybe it was just supposed to teach you a lesson. Accepting that feels good.

Remember: Keep It Fresh

Have an open mind—about who you are and how you're changing and about the world around you. Teachers come in all forms. Knowledge comes to us from people and places we don't expect, and if we're not open to it, we won't gather it. Knowledge is never a waste. Every piece of knowledge that you gain on this journey of life is going to be useful to you in some way.

affirmation practice

Say this affirmation several times upon waking in the morning and before going to bed at night:

I am capable of getting through tough times as I get stronger mentally, spiritually, and physically every day.

CHAPTER SEVEN

Your Mind Is a Muscle

The more you train your body, the stronger it gets. You may not see results as quickly as you'd like, but you *are* getting results. Each rep, each workout is adding power and definition. The same is true of your mind: the more you train it, the stronger it gets. Changing your thought patterns won't happen overnight. One gym session doesn't make you super fit, right? But saying affirmations each day—positive statements of how you want to feel expressed as if you already felt that way—strengthens your mind and reinforces these positive thoughts. Hopefully, you've already begun to experience the power of affirmations by using the ones I suggest at the start of each chapter. Now it's time to create your own affirmations. Only by creating your own will you tap in to the true depth of their power. Start using your own personal affirmations, and over time, you will grow stronger. In order to eliminate unconscious negative thought patterns, a consistent stream of new thoughts must be introduced on a regular basis.

Affirmations become even more powerful and likely to manifest when your chakras, your body's energy centers, are balanced. Like my yoga and meditation practice, checking in with my chakras is another way of going within to work things out. If my chakras are balanced, I know I'm putting out positive energy into the world that will attract what I am hoping to bring into my life. If I find that my chakras are unbalanced, I have specific, practical actions I can take to get them back into balance. Let me show you how to become aware of your chakras and keep your energy flowing smoothly.

BALANCE YOUR CHAKRAS

Chakras are the body's energy centers that help regulate all its processes. There are seven chakras, positioned from the base of the spine to the top of the head. Each one has its own vibrational frequency and color, controls a specific bodily function, and influences certain emotions. Getting to know your chakras, being able to identify when they are blocked, and learning how to remove that blockage are foundational skills for self-knowledge. Like meditation and yoga, your chakras connect you with your spiritual self. When energy is flowing freely through your chakras, your body, mind, and soul are in alignment, and the voice of your authentic self is clear as a bell. Blocked chakras cause physical discomfort or pain and emotional distress. As you start to use affirmations and visualizations to manifest the life you most desire (described a little later in this book), you'll find that this process will be much easier when your chakras are balanced.

Use the following descriptions of the seven chakras, along with the quizzes I've designed, to identify where you may have an imbalance, and then use my tips to restore optimal energy flow. The crystals and essential oils associated with each chakra can also help (see the chart on page 99). As you go through each chakra, visualize that chakra's energy center and color spinning clockwise (the term chakra is Sanskrit for "wheel").

the 7 main chakras

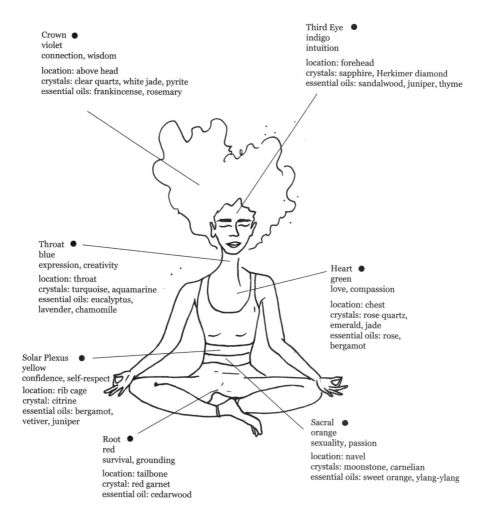

Crown ●
violet
connection, wisdom

location: above head
crystals: clear quartz, white jade, pyrite
essential oils: frankincense, rosemary

Third Eye ●
indigo
intuition

location: forehead
crystals: sapphire, Herkimer diamond
essential oils: sandalwood, juniper, thyme

Throat ●
blue
expression, creativity

location: throat
crystals: turquoise, aquamarine
essential oils: eucalyptus,
lavender, chamomile

Heart ●
green
love, compassion

location: chest
crystals: rose quartz,
emerald, jade
essential oils: rose,
bergamot

Solar Plexus ●
yellow
confidence, self-respect
location: rib cage
crystal: citrine
essential oils: bergamot,
vetiver, juniper

Root ●
red
survival, grounding

location: tailbone
crystal: red garnet
essential oil: cedarwood

Sacral ●
orange
sexuality, passion

location: navel
crystals: moonstone, carnelian
essential oils: sweet orange, ylang-ylang

ROOT CHAKRA

The root chakra is located at the base of your tailbone. It is the seat of physical vitality and the fundamental urge to survive. Take the following quiz to determine if you have an imbalance in this chakra.

Answer Yes or No

Yes ☐ No ☐   I exercise regularly.

Yes ☐ No ☐   My diet is healthy and balanced most of the time.

Yes ☐ No ☐   I take time to be in nature on a regular basis.

Yes ☐ No ☐   I feel good about my body.

Yes ☐ No ☐   I am well organized.

Yes ☐ No ☐   It's easy to stay focused on what I am doing.

Yes ☐ No ☐   I'm comfortable with my level of prosperity and abundance.

Yes ☐ No ☐   I usually trust my instincts.

Yes ☐ No ☐   I'm good at taking care of details.

Yes ☐ No ☐   I regularly declutter.

If you answered NO to more than three or four statements, it may indicate that you have an imbalance in the root chakra.

Balanced Root Chakra: Having a balanced root chakra will help you to feel comfortable in your own skin. You will have a healthy attitude toward your body and will be in good physical health. You will be well grounded. When things don't go your way in life, you will be able to stand on your own two feet and work things out. In general, you are a stable person who is in touch with your natural instincts.

Overactive Root Chakra: If you have an overactive root chakra, you may find that you tend to be addicted to food. Physically, you may be overweight. This extra weight (both physically and energetically) leaves you feeling lethargic and heavy. You may be overly materialistic, or you may be driven by greed, which is really about your insecurity regarding money and survival. You tend to have a hoarding mentality and can be obsessive about routine. You tend to dislike change or anything that upsets your sense of security.

Underactive Root Chakra: If your root chakra is deficient in energy, you may be underweight and very ungrounded. You may have a fearful and restless nature that makes you scattered and unfocused and means it is hard for you to meet your commitments. You may also find yourself plagued by constant financial worries and lack a sense of security, probably changing jobs often. You live predominantly in a fantasy world and tend to be vague.

5 Tips for Balancing Your Root Chakra

1. Create a clean and organized home environment. Try to create order and structure in your life and home (e.g., filing, clearing out cupboards, etc.).

2. Spend as much time as possible in healthy environments, especially nature. Find time to walk, or dance, barefoot on the earth.

3. Find a form of exercise that really suits you, and carry it out in a balanced way. Learn to listen to your body's needs. Know the signs of an illness coming on or when you need to take a break.

4. Eat healthily, and mindfully, and ensure that you are getting the right vitamins, minerals, and nutrients for your body.

5. Limit the amount of toxins you put into your body. This includes alcohol and drugs but also the toxins in the food you eat, the chemicals in your cleaning products, and the products you put on your skin.

SACRAL CHAKRA

The sacral chakra, located in your navel, is the energy center of relationships, where we develop an inward sense of self and an outward awareness of the feelings of others. Take the following quiz to determine if you have an imbalance in this chakra.

Answer Yes or No

Yes ☐ No ☐ I'm in touch with my feelings and find it easy to express my emotions.

Yes ☐ No ☐ I enjoy healthy, intimate relationships.

Yes ☐ No ☐ I am in touch with my own sensual nature.

Yes ☐ No ☐ I regularly do activities that I find pleasurable.

Yes ☐ No ☐ I have things that I am passionate about in my life.

Yes ☐ No ☐ I can identify what my needs are.

Yes ☐ No ☐ I love to dance; moving with music makes me feel good.

Yes ☐ No ☐ I make time for myself to relax and feel good.

Yes ☐ No ☐ I'm comfortable embracing changes in my life.

Yes ☐ No ☐ I enjoy taking baths or swimming.

If you answered NO to more than three or four statements, it may indicate that you have an imbalance in the sacral chakra.

Balanced Sacral Chakra: When your sacral chakra is balanced, you will be able to express your emotions without them overwhelming you. You will enjoy healthy sexual relationships and will be in touch with your own sensuality. You find it easy to nurture yourself with the simple pleasures of rest, good food, and quality time with loved ones. You will be in touch with your inner feminine energy (whether you are male or female) and easily able to surrender to the flow of life.

Overactive Sacral Chakra: An excess of energy in the sacral chakra is characterized by someone who lives in constant emotional turmoil. If you have an overactive sacral chakra, you may experience frequent mood swings and constantly get caught up in the drama of life. You may be clingy in relationships and emotionally oversensitive. You are a highly sensual person with strong urges that are usually acted out in a sexual way. You can also be manipulative and overly dependent on others for emotional support. Finally, you have a tendency to overindulge in life's pleasures and live extravagantly.

Underactive Sacral Chakra: If the sacral chakra is lacking energy or underactive, you may experience sexual dysfunction and repressed sexual desires. You may find it difficult to allow any form of pleasure into your life, and therefore, you may lack passion and excitement. As you have a tendency to block your emotions, you may feel empty and lonely, finding it difficult to form close relationships. You may also display signs of pessimism and extreme introversion.

5 Tips for Balancing Your Sacral Chakra

1. Get support for any emotional issues going on in your life. This may include finding a form of therapy, such as counseling or energetic healing.

2. Try not to keep feelings bottled up, but seek out safe ways to express and release emotions, perhaps by talking to a friend, dancing, painting, or writing in a journal.

3. Find a regular practice to help keep you emotionally balanced, such as meditation, yoga, or relaxation exercises.

4. Create opportunities for pleasurable feelings in your life. Find the time to do things you really enjoy, such as getting a massage or cooking a beautiful meal. Create some "me time" every day.

5. Create an emotionally calming environment in your home by cleansing your personal space with incense and burning candles. Spend your time with positive and uplifting people.

SOLAR PLEXUS CHAKRA

The solar plexus chakra, located between your rib cage, is the center of a strong sense of self and self-esteem. Take the following quiz to determine if you have an imbalance in this chakra.

Answer Yes or No

Yes ☐ No ☐   I feel confident in most situations.

Yes ☐ No ☐   I am able to laugh easily.

Yes ☐ No ☐   I see projects and commitments through to completion.

Yes ☐ No ☐   I have the courage to take risks when necessary.

Yes ☐ No ☐   I establish appropriate boundaries for myself.

Yes ☐ No ☐   I stand up for myself when I need to.

Yes ☐ No ☐   I am in the career that feels right for me.

Yes ☐ No ☐   I can make my own decisions with ease.

Yes ☐ No ☐   I usually feel like I have enough energy to do what I need to do.

Yes ☐ No ☐   I have a clear sense of the direction I want to go in.

If you answered NO to more than three or four statements, it may indicate that you have an imbalance in the solar plexus chakra.

Balanced Solar Plexus Chakra: A balanced solar plexus chakra allows you to have a strong sense of self-worth. You feel confident and have a good sense of your own personal power. You understand that power is not something you have over others or allow someone else to take away from you but is an inner strength that you can always draw on when needed. You enjoy spontaneity, trying new things, and taking on new challenges. There is laughter in your life, and you are in touch with your inner masculinity (whether you are male or female).

Overactive Solar Plexus Chakra: An excess of energy in this chakra is experienced in overly aggressive behavior. You may dominate others, be unyielding in your opinions, and be stubborn in your outlook on life. You might also have a tendency to be overly competitive and arrogant and display controlling tendencies. This can lead to obsessive pursuits fueled by your iron will and the need to be constantly busy. You seek validation for your success and outward accomplishments.

Underactive Solar Plexus Chakra: An underactive solar plexus chakra may mean that you experience low energy levels, which can lead to a lack of spontaneity in your life. You may be weak-willed and allow other people to walk all over you. You are often shy and withdrawn and avoid situations where you may be the center of attention. You tend to be undisciplined and can display passive-aggressive behavior as you end up doing things because you can't say no. You avoid taking risks, have a very serious outlook, and can suffer from bouts of depression.

5 Tips for Balancing Your Solar Plexus Chakra

1. Try to take responsibility for your life and not blame others, circumstances, or the universe for the challenges and disappointments you face.

2. Keep sight of your own unique direction, ambitions, and goals. Take the right action to achieve these goals, even if it is one small step at a time.

3. Find self-discipline in your life.

4. Focus on creating good boundaries.

5. Celebrate your achievements and successes.

HEART CHAKRA

The heart chakra, located in your chest, is the center of unconditional love and spiritual growth. Take the following quiz to determine if you have an imbalance in this chakra.

Answer Yes or No

Yes ☐ No ☐   I am a generous person.

Yes ☐ No ☐   I have open, honest relationships.

Yes ☐ No ☐   I am kind to myself.

Yes ☐ No ☐   I forgive easily.

Yes ☐ No ☐   I empathize easily with other living beings.

Yes ☐ No ☐   I accept myself as I am.

Yes ☐ No ☐   I have a lot of joy in my life.

Yes ☐ No ☐   I am comfortable with both giving and receiving.

Yes ☐ No ☐   I feel genuine happiness for others.

Yes ☐ No ☐   I can own my part in any conflicts I have with others.

If you answered NO to more than three or four statements, it may indicate that you have an imbalance in the heart chakra.

Balanced Heart Chakra: When your heart chakra is balanced, you have an open and compassionate attitude toward yourself and other people. You can easily form intimate and loving relationships. You are a generous person and are able to be there for people without feeling you have to fix them, or their situation, in any way. You move through life with a lightness and openness that has a deep effect upon others. You also have a balanced outlook on life. You are not judgmental and don't bear grudges. Forgiveness comes easily to you. Life feels joyful.

Overactive Heart Chakra: When the energy in the heart chakra is excessive, you may experience feelings of jealousy and possessiveness. If you are lacking in self-love and acceptance, an overriding hunger for connection with others results in co-dependent relationships. You seek constant validation for love outside of yourself. This may lead to excessive caregiving, which you hope will earn you the right to be loved.

Underactive Heart Chakra: A deficiency in this chakra may be the result of a broken heart. If this is the case, your heart chakra may be underactive, causing you to withdraw from people and become quite cold and distant as a way of protecting your heart. You may find it difficult to forgive and let go of old hurts, and therefore, you remain stuck in the past. Because you are afraid to feel, you lose touch with others and struggle to find empathy for both others and yourself. You may display a cynical and bitter outlook toward life and can be quite judgmental of people you meet as a way of creating distance between yourself and others.

5 Tips for Balancing Your Heart Chakra

1. Find compassion and kindness for yourself daily so that it is possible to find it for others.

2. See beyond people's behaviors and through to the real person.

3. Live your life in the most generous and open way that you can.

4. Know that compassion does not mean that you have to fix things; just being present for another person is healing.

5. Do your best to be nonjudgmental of yourself or others. If you find yourself judging others, breathe into your heart, and let the judgment go with your out-breath.

THROAT CHAKRA

The throat chakra, located in your throat, is the center of communication and creativity. Take the following quiz to determine if you have an imbalance in this chakra.

Answer Yes or No

Yes ☐ No ☐   I am a good listener.

Yes ☐ No ☐   I have a good sense of rhythm.

Yes ☐ No ☐   I have a strong, clear voice.

Yes ☐ No ☐   I naturally express my creativity.

Yes ☐ No ☐   I feel comfortable speaking my truth.

Yes ☐ No ☐   I pick up on vibes easily.

Yes ☐ No ☐   I feel like I am able to just be myself with people.

Yes ☐ No ☐   I make time for some silence in my life.

Yes ☐ No ☐   I feel grateful for my life.

Yes ☐ No ☐   I have a good sense of timing. I know when to speak and when not to.

If you answered NO to more than three or four statements, it may indicate that you have an imbalance in the throat chakra.

Balanced Throat Chakra: When your throat chakra is balanced, you have good, clear communication and are able to express yourself authentically. You live your life by your own truth. Your creative life is important to you, and you find it easy to authentically express yourself. On a more subtle level, you are tuned in to the vibrations around you. You resonate with your life—where you live, what you do, the people you spend time with. As well as being a good listener to others, you also listen to your inner voice. Your life feels harmonious.

Overactive Throat Chakra: If your throat chakra is overactive, you tend to be an incessant talker. You are probably not a very good listener and may have a tendency to dominate conversations with others. Often what you say has little relevance to those you are speaking with, or you go overboard sharing details. You may also enjoy gossip and have a tendency to complain or speak negatively of others. You find it difficult to connect with your own creativity.

Underactive Throat Chakra: Alternatively, if your throat chakra is deficient in energy and is underactive, you may find it difficult to express your true feelings, as you feel you can never find the right words. If you have a small, meek voice that lacks resonance and have a fear of speaking, then you may have a deficiency in your throat chakra. You probably feel shy and quite withdrawn from the world, as you struggle to engage others in conversation. It sometimes feels like you are wearing a mask when you are with others. You find it difficult to express your creativity.

5 Tips for Balancing Your Throat Chakra

1. Have the intention of always being open and honest with your communication. Try to keep communication meaningful, not indulging in gossip, lies, and pointless chitchat.

2. Be mindful of the Buddhist precept of wise speech: "Is it true? Is it kind? Is it necessary? Is it the right time?"

3. Acknowledge that listening is as much a part of communication as talking, and practice active listening.

4. Be open to higher levels of communication (telepathy, clairvoyance, channeling).

5. Explore ways of connecting with your innate, authentic creativity (singing, dancing, painting, cooking, personal style, etc.).

THIRD EYE CHAKRA

The third eye chakra, located in your forehead, is the center of intuition. The opening of the third eye corresponds with spiritual awakening. Take the following quiz to determine if you have an imbalance in this chakra.

Answer Yes or No

Yes ☐ No ☐   I trust my intuition.

Yes ☐ No ☐   I act on the guidance I receive.

Yes ☐ No ☐   I remember my dreams easily.

Yes ☐ No ☐   I have a good memory.

Yes ☐ No ☐   I can visualize easily.

Yes ☐ No ☐   I trust the signs and synchronicities that show up in my life.

Yes ☐ No ☐   I am open to psychic experiences.

Yes ☐ No ☐   I value the power of my imagination.

Yes ☐ No ☐   I have original ideas and take the steps
needed to bring them to life.

Yes ☐ No ☐   I am able to look at the bigger picture of
my life when I need to.

If you answered NO to more than three or four statements, it
may indicate that you have an imbalance in the third eye chakra.

Balanced Third Eye Chakra: You are able to clearly see what
you want out of life as you have a well-developed inner vision.
You are in touch with your intuition and trust the insights you
receive. You may have psychic abilities or a strong connection
with your sixth sense. You value the importance of your imagination and have a good memory that allows you to easily remember details when you need them. You recognize the importance of your dreams. Not only do you remember them, you also
value their messages. You often find yourself in the right place
at the right time.

Overactive Third Eye Chakra: An excess of energy in the third
eye is most obviously demonstrated by nightmares, obsessive
fantasies, and hallucinations. A feeling of having lost touch
with reality may accompany your waking hours. This is a result
of too much psychic input that you are unable to ground. This
may lead to feeling paranoid and superstitious.

Underactive Third Eye Chakra: Alternatively, deficiency in
the third eye chakra is reflected in an inability to recall your
dreams, poor memory, and difficulty in visualizing. You may
also feel quite out of touch with your intuition and fail to pick
up on signs and synchronicities. This manifests through difficulties in finding alternative solutions to problems and becoming overdependent on your rational mind.

5 Tips for Balancing Your Third Eye Chakra

1. Commit to regular practice of intuition-building exercises (meditation, guided visualization, dreamwork).

2. Regularly ask advice from your intuitive self, and then be open to the flow of intuition.

3. Recognize the relevance of chance encounters, coincidences, and synchronicities. See these as signposts to guide you.

4. Use your imagination to create the life you want. Use visualization, or create a vision board.

5. Learn to trust your "sixth sense." When it feels appropriate, use intuition even if the sources of your feelings are beyond rational explanation.

CROWN CHAKRA

The crown chakra, located above your head, represents the highest level of consciousness and enlightenment. It integrates all of the chakras and their respective qualities. Take the following quiz to determine if you have an imbalance in this chakra.

Answer Yes or No

Yes ☐ No ☐ I regularly meditate or make time for self-reflection.

Yes ☐ No ☐ I have a relationship with my own source of spirituality.

Yes ☐ No ☐ I have a sense of sacredness in my daily life.

Yes ☐ No ☐ I truly know that my soul has a life beyond the constraints of my body.

Yes ☐ No ☐ I often slow down and notice the wonder around me.

Yes ☐ No ☐ I regularly find gratitude for what I have.

Yes ☐ No ☐ I pray or ask for higher help when
I need it.

Yes ☐ No ☐ I bring my spirituality into my daily life.

Yes ☐ No ☐ I feel like I am living my soul's purpose.

Yes ☐ No ☐ I feel connected to a universal consciousness
beyond that which is mine alone.

If you answered NO to more than three or four statements, it may indicate that you have an imbalance in the crown chakra.

Balanced Crown Chakra: Your crown chakra is balanced when your sense of self feels connected to the world and to the realm beyond. You are connected to the spiritual aspect of human existence and live your life soulfully. You live in the present, which releases you from the past and allows you to stop worrying about the future. Your life feels sacred, and you are able to find value and depth in the simplest of your daily experiences.

Overactive Crown Chakra: If your crown chakra is overactive, you may feel quite dissociated from your body. Usually, as a result of your spiritual addiction (used as an escape), you deny your physical needs. You may eat poorly, neglect your comfort, or struggle with poverty in pursuit of loftier aims. You may exist in a world dominated by spiritual visions but be unable to integrate your spirituality into your everyday life. On another level, you may overintellectualize as you search for the meaning of life. You may be preoccupied with knowledge at the expense of having any real experience and understanding of the world around you.

Underactive Crown Chakra: An underactive crown chakra may result in a limited worldview. If your crown chakra is closed, you may have very rigid belief systems and show minimal regard for anything of a spiritual nature. It may be easy for you to become consumed by material concerns and closed off from more meaningful experiences. You are rarely open to new ideas, as these may challenge your belief systems, and you find the need to constantly demonstrate that your ideas are right.

5 Tips for Balancing Your Crown Chakra

1. Practice meditation or relaxation daily (even if only for a few brief minutes). This helps quiet the mind, making the connection to Spirit more accessible.

2. Develop your own relationship with Spirit, whether this be with God, Allah, the Universe, angels, spirit guides, or whatever higher source you acknowledge. Trust what feels right for you.

3. Regularly ask for higher guidance, and let these spiritual forces guide you. Remain open to inspiration (when you become inspired, you are in Spirit).

4. Commit to your own spiritual practice. Some people find this connection through religion and visit churches or temples to enhance their spiritual experiences. For others, this connection to Spirit is found in nature and attuning to the beauty and the wonderment of all that is. Whether you find it surfing a wave as you connect with the vastness of the ocean, meditating in your living room, hiking to the top of a mountain, or participating in a ritual or ceremony, it really doesn't matter. It is experiencing a spiritual connection that is important.

5. Try to embody spiritual lessons in your everyday life, and give regular thanks.

JUST DO IT

After my college track injury, I was consumed by negativity. My body had failed me, and my whole life was out of whack. I felt worthless. In a bookstore, I spotted *You Can Heal Your Life* by Louise Hay. The title resonated with me deeply. I *needed* to heal my life. I thought, *Okay, why not? Maybe this will help.* Her ideas on the power of thought and the power of affirmations appealed to me. So I started saying a few affirmations each morning:

I am Loved.

I am Worthy.

I am Healthy.

Is this really going to work? I thought. I wasn't sure, but I decided to commit to the practice because something had to work. I didn't want to be injured, and I didn't want to continue having negative thoughts that I knew were not serving me. I would try and see.

Over time, I started to feel better and better. My negative thoughts were slowly turning into positive thoughts, and those positive thoughts were building my confidence and making me feel better about myself and my situation. As my confidence grew, my yoga practice got better, and as my yoga practice got better, my mood got better. One positive feeling led to the next, and the good in my life just kept growing. I had more compassion and patience; I was willing to try more new things; I didn't give up on myself; I poured more into myself.

Now I say affirmations twice daily. I wouldn't start or end my day without them. Many of my affirmations have remained the same since college, but over time, I've added more mature ones that speak to a specific need. Some of my affirmations are these:

I am Loved.	I am Abundant.
I am Worthy.	I am willing to let go.
I am Healthy.	I won't love anyone to
I am Wealthy.	the detriment of myself.
I am Wise.	

The "Get Loved Up Morning Prayer" that opens this book (page x) is based on the affirmations I live by.

Create an Affirmation

Write an affirmation to repeat to yourself each day this week. Make it powerful. Where do you feel weak? What area of your life is causing you stress? Write an affirmation to help you feel stronger. For example:

I am more than my fears.

I can tap in to a wellspring of inner strength at any time.

I approve of myself and love myself deeply and completely.

I am proud of myself for trying to overcome my fears.

By creating your own affirmation, truly believing in it, and feeling it to be true, you will realize it.

Mirror Work

Look in the mirror as you say your affirmations. Affirming these positive statements to yourself as you view your image, especially if you gaze into your eyes, is a powerful way of reinforcing them. There's a reason the eyes are called the windows of the soul! Do mirror work every morning and in the evening before you go to bed.

CHANGE YOUR THOUGHTS; CHANGE YOUR REALITY

Think of one of your affirmations. Hold it in your mind. How does it look in real life? How does it feel? For example, if your affirmation is "I am loved," what does that look like to you? What are you doing? Who are you with? Create strong feelings around the words. Feelings, more than just the words, attract what you desire. If the reason you come up with for saying these words is "because Koya told me to say it," you really don't feel that they're true. If you really don't feel it in your heart, your affirmation—and the likelihood of it manifesting—is weakened. Try using visualization again with another affirmation and see how it resonates.

Some people view affirmations as misleading or inauthentic. They ask, *How can I say "I am confident" when I'm feeling timid and uncertain? It's not true. I'm not feeling confident. I'm actually feeling quite insecure right now. Am I telling the truth by saying "I am confident"?*

Affirmations are not about truth telling. Affirmations are about optimism and attracting what you really want, starting in your mind. Make it true in your mind. Whether it's true in reality *right now* doesn't matter. If you want to change your reality, you have to think differently. Otherwise, you attract more and more of what you already have. If you want to remain feeling timid and uncertain, you will in an unconscious way keep saying that to yourself. But if you want to start feeling confident, you have to change your thoughts.

Or perhaps your limiting belief is "I'll never run a successful business." If you keep that in mind, you'll never be successful because you think that statement is true. Start with a simple affirmation: "I am successful." *Feel* what that means to you. Are your shoulders hunched and tight or relaxed? Is your mind clear and confident? Is your mood upbeat? Feel that success in every fiber of your being. Even though you don't have that dream business in front of you right now, by starting to really believe that success is possible, one day you will have it.

There is energetic power in an affirmation! Saying it, believing it, and feeling it to be true changes the energy around you and raises your vibration. By changing your vibration from what you *don't* want to what you *do* want, you'll be in alignment energetically and attract more people, places, and things that are also in alignment with that energy—and your end goal—to you.

Do what makes your soul sing. Live a life filled with passion, and commit to doing more of what you love.

yoga practice:
downward-facing dog pose to plank pose

- Lie on your stomach.
- Bring your hands under your shoulders, and spread your fingers wide.
- Bring your feet hip-width apart and curl your toes under.
- Push into the floor, and come to your knees with an inhale, then slowly straighten your legs with an exhale.

- Release your heels toward the floor.
- Reach your tailbone toward the sky behind you to lengthen your spine.
- Bring your head in between your arms.

- Shift forward with an inhale, aligning your shoulders over your wrists.
- Engage your core and legs.
- Gaze toward the floor.
- Hold the pose and take slow, deep breaths.
- Push back to Downward-Facing Dog with an exhale.

Modification: Lower your knees to the floor.

BE CLEAR AND CONSISTENT

An affirmation isn't a guarantee that you will get exactly what you want. It will attract what is in alignment with your energy. But the more clearly you articulate your goals in your thoughts, the better the results. The more confident, more certain, more dedicated, and more committed you are to your affirmation and changing your present reality, the higher the quality of the results you will experience. By putting more energy toward the reality you want, you attract more of that positive energy to you. Again, it's like going to the gym. Your mind is a muscle. If you half lift or do 10 reps instead of 20, you might see some results, but you won't get the same results as if you went 100 percent.

Part of giving 100 percent of your energy is being consistent and saying your affirmations every day. You can't just write down an affirmation one day and expect it to work. You have to say them every day, preferably in the morning and in the evening. If you go to the gym once a week, you're really not building on anything. You're going, and it's hard, and then you stop. If you say affirmations once a week, you don't really have much to build on, either. The power of affirmations is felt when you make saying them a daily practice. Consistently saying the words and feeling your new reality will attract the energy to support your ideal situation.

meditation practice

Follow the numbered meditation instructions on pages 14–15 and use the following as your intention:

I am capable of getting through tough times as I get stronger mentally, spiritually, and physically every day. I am strong enough to stop and listen to my inner voice of wisdom and guidance.

Remember: You Are What You Think

You are your thoughts. Your life stems from your thoughts. Think in ways that benefit you. Use affirmations to raise your vibration and attract what you most desire.

affirmation practice

Say this affirmation several times upon waking in the morning and before going to bed at night:

I can see all of my needs being met as I flow through my days with ease and grace.

CHAPTER EIGHT

Visualize Your New Reality

Visualization is one of the most powerful ways to manifest your ideal reality. It helps you to keep your mind's eye on your heart's desires. Once you've identified what you want your world to look like, visualization can help you to imagine it exactly as it would appear in your day-to-day life. What does your dream house look like? Your ideal job? Your most epic vacation? Seeing yourself precisely where you want to be will keep you motivated, especially when distractions arise. Visualization is so powerful, I suggest practicing it daily, either when you wake up or before you go to bed.

In earlier chapters, we touched on using visualization to help heal trauma and to feel your affirmations as real. Remember, feelings, more than just words, attract what you desire. Here our visualization practice gets more targeted, with specialized techniques to help you imagine the emotions, experiences, people, and things you want to bring into your life, to feel their presence and increase their likelihood of manifesting.

You Are Here to Glow

In order to attract new, positive people, things, and experiences into your life, you need to be vibrating at the highest possible level. When you feel strong, confident, and loved, everything is open to you; everything is possible. If you feel down and depressed or filled with negative emotions, nothing about your life will change. When you allow a situation or person to get you down, you're vibrating at a low frequency. Unless you start to focus on the positive feelings you want to have in your life, you can be down for a long time.

The key to attraction is to change those negative feelings into positive ones and raise your vibration. If you don't do that, none of the other techniques and practices I've shared with you will have a lasting impact. Visualization is an effective way to get unstuck from those negative feelings.

I want you to know these things:

- The universe is for you, not against you.
- You are not here to fail or to be miserable.
- You are here to glow and shine like the moon and the sun.
- You can shine in the darkness and shine in the light.

Unsticking negative feelings is a major challenge for a lot of people, especially those who experience depression, as I sometimes do. I'm very sensitive and empathic, so I feel intensely. Hurt cuts me deep. There have been times when I haven't wanted to live, when I've wanted to kill myself. Generally, I view my emotional sensitivity as a blessing because it enables me to be deeply compassionate and help others in a profound way. But sometimes, when I'm overwhelmed by negative emotions, it feels like a curse. Visualization has helped me to move out of those feelings much more quickly.

yoga practice: hero pose

When you're depressed, it can be easy to feel stuck in one place. Yoga is a great way to keep moving forward. A loss or breakup often stalls us. You may want to wait for the pain to go away, but you have to keep going. Yoga shows you how to get back up and keep moving. It may look like you're sitting still in Hero Pose, but your body is *working*. You will feel a stretch in your knees, ankles, and thighs. Hero Pose improves posture and should make you more aware of how your breath moves through your body.

- Sit with your legs folded underneath you.

- Lift your hips, and open your feet a few inches to either side.

- Carefully sit in between your feet.
- Use your hands to pull your calves up and out so that your bottom is snuggled in between your feet.
- Point your toes behind you.
- Rest your hands on your thighs.
- Lengthen your spine.
- Close your eyes.
- Hold the pose and take slow, deep breaths.
- Carefully lift your bottom with an inhale, then swing your legs to one side to return to sitting.

Modification: Sit on top of a block or bolster placed between your feet.

RAISE YOUR VIBRATION WITH MUSIC

Listening to affirming, upbeat music is one of my favorite ways to raise my vibration and shift my feelings. Music is so powerful; when it expresses the way I want to feel, it raises my energy immediately. It doesn't matter what style of music it is—hip-hop, jazz, or rock. What does matter is that the sound and especially the lyrics affirm the way you want to feel. Listening to a melancholy breakup song isn't going to help you feel less sad over the end of a relationship; it's only going to validate your sadness.

After a long, exhausting day of auditions, I found out that I didn't make it to the next round of tryouts for *American Idol*. Then, Pink's "So What" blasted through the loudspeakers. Whether it was serendipitous or strategic—those producers had hundreds of angsty singers on their hands—that song lifted me right up. I thought, *So what if I didn't get this; I'm still great. I'm amazing and beautiful. It's okay.* I continue to turn to that song and so many others to help me deal with failure and rejection and raise my vibration.

Music can also help you cope with other people's negative emotions. A couple of years ago, after a frantic rush to get to the airport, all I wanted to do was sink into my seat on the plane and relax for a few hours. Not to be. A woman with hostile eyes who was seated in my row demanded that instead of taking my assigned spot, I should find a seat in another row since the plane wasn't full. I agreed to move to the window seat so that she could sit next to her daughter and she'd have more room, but I was not going to wander around the plane, trying to find another seat when I had a perfectly good one already. She did not like that. Her color was up, her eyes were rolling, and the insults were pouring from her mouth. It's probably a good thing they were in a language I couldn't understand.

I put on my headphones to drown her out, but being an empath and very sensitive to energy, I felt her rage on a soul level. I closed my eyes and tried to be still. I played my favorite mantra music from the band Beautiful Chorus and immediately felt calmer and more balanced. Even so, I couldn't completely relax or fall asleep. I sensed profound sadness in the woman next to me, and I opened my eyes to find her in tears. I reached out to her, and with just a little bit of gentle kindness and concern, I got her to open up. Her youngest daughter had just died, and she felt grief and guilt at missing the opportunity to make peace with her after they'd had an argument. She mentioned that her daughter's name was Angel, and when I shared that my nickname was Angel, I said, "I forgive you; I love you." She gave me a warm, motherly hug and whispered, "It's Angel, thank you!" We talked like best friends for the rest of the flight.

I never would have been able to connect with her or comfort her if I'd stayed frustrated. Music helped make that possible.

Make Your Own Motivational Playlist

Create your own motivational playlist. Choose whatever genre of music you like. I suggest creating two: one playlist with music that contains lyrics and one with music that does not. Instrumental music frees your mind and opens your heart to receive messages from your soul that I call Divine Downloads. The Get Loved Up prayer (see page x) was a Divine Download. I was listening to my favorite instrumental yoga playlist, and it just came to me. I wrote it in Notes on my phone and now have the students of my yoga teacher training commit it to memory because I feel it has blessed my life and focused my mind-set on living in a vibration of love.

I love to make playlists. Music is a very powerful tool to help feelings manifest. Here are two of my motivational playlists:

Instrumental

Affelaye, "Want Me," in *Maybe There*

—

Essáy, "Lyla," in *Ocarina EP*

—

Hermitude, "HyperParadise," in *HyperParadise*

—

ODESZA, "IPlayYouListen," in *Summer's Gone*

—

Killigrew, "Lumina," in *Lumina*

—

Michael St. Laurent, "Reverie," in *Reverie*

—

Bearson, "Pink Medicine," in *Pink Medicine*

—

Kacy Hill, "Foreign Fields," in *Bloo*

—

Finding Hope, "Wonder," in *Wonder*

—

Pretty Lights, "One Day They'll Know (ODESZA Remix)," in *A Color Map of the Sun (Remixes)*

—

CMA, "Ethereal," in *Open Your Eyes EP*

—

ODESZA, "Sun Models (feat. Madelyn Grant)," in *In Return*

—

Hoodboi, "Palm Reader (feat. Lido)," in *Palm Reader*

—

East Forest, "Soul Speak," in *Music to Die To*

—

Sol Rising, "Your Love (Instrumental)," in *The Chillout Sessions*

With Lyrics

India.Arie, "I Am Light," in *SongVersation: Medicine*

—

Jamila Woods, "Holy," in *HEAVN*

—

Stwo, "Lovin U," in *Majestic Casual—Chapter 1*

—

Jhené Aiko, "Frequency," in *Trip*

—

Sophia Black, "Vibration," in *Vibration*

—

Jill Scott, "Golden," in *Beautifully Human: Words and Sounds Vol. 2*

—

Clean Bandit & Jess Glynne, "Real Love—The Chainsmokers Remix," in *Real Love (Remixes)*

—

Ibeyi, "River," in *Ibeyi*

—

Seinabo Sey, "Still," in *Pretend*

—

JMR, "Closer," in *Ritual*

—

mAsis, "Make Me Higher," in *Kennesaw*

—

James Bay, "Let It Go," in *Chaos and the Calm*

—

Goapele, "Closer," in *Even Closer*

—

Beautiful Chorus, "I'm All I Need," in *Mantras in Love*

—

Jennifer Hudson & Tori Kelly, "Hallelujah," in *Sing (Original Motion Picture Soundtrack)*

—

Jai-Jagdeesh, "In Dreams," in *Of Heaven & Earth*

BE LOVED

Music has such a powerful influence on my feelings that I wanted to write and share a song that would spread positivity and love in the world. "Be Loved" expresses everything I stand for: loving myself, others, and this beautiful planet. Love is present in everything around you, and your life is so valuable.

"Be Loved"

Everybody's searching for something to fill that empty space.

The hollow heart is reaching out for one to lead the way.

Would you follow passion if it could free you? Are we chasing shadows to avoid reflections of a past that can't erase? Waiting for an answer from the sky, searching for yourself.

Look inside.

Breathe.

It takes time.

Promises break and people change, one thing remains the same. Everybody wants to be Loved, to be Loved, to be Loved, to be Loved.

Like a rose plucked from the garden, my tears dried, petals have fallen. They lead me to beautiful places in me.

Would you follow passion if it could free you? Are we chasing shadows to avoid reflection of a past that can't erase? Waiting for an answer from the sky, searching for yourself.

Look inside.

Breathe.

It takes time.

Promises break and people change, one thing remains the same. Everybody wants to be Loved, to be Loved.

DREAM JUICY

Commit 100 percent to your ideal reality. Not someone else's reality. Whatever you're thinking should be so good, so great, and so juicy that you get uncomfortable. When I asked one of my clients to think of her ideal reality, she said, "I'm actually feeling kind of nauseous." That's perfect! You're thinking big enough. You're pushing your limits. Scared, super nervous, shaking? Now you're dreaming; now you're putting it out there. If you're not scared, you're playing it safe.

Think outside of the box and outside of your comfort zone. Let your mind and your creativity run free. That's where you'll find a dream that is truly in alignment with your soul.

I have always wanted an ocean-view home. The first time I visited the seaside neighborhood of Marina del Rey, I knew that was the place for me. It felt good to be there. The vibe, the people, everything about it suited me. But when I first moved to California, there was no way I could afford it. So I rented what I could afford—a tiny little room in someone else's house in Marina del Rey. I slept on a mattress stacked on top of two storage containers and worked at a computer desk. That was all that small space could fit and all I had to my name. But I was determined. I knew that if I worked hard enough and saved every penny, I'd get myself a place in Marina del Rey. After three months of working my butt off, I had just enough money for the first and last month's rent and deposit to rent a studio apartment.

A humble little studio near the water would have suited me just fine and that's what I told the housing specialist who I contacted to show me apartments. Even though I made it clear that I didn't want to see places I couldn't afford, he insisted we take a look at a one-bedroom apartment renting for a little above my budget.

"There's no harm in looking," he said, "especially if it's only $300 over your price range. It's a really rare deal." We went to go see it, and I loved it as soon as I walked in. It was so beautiful with a huge walk-in closet and cute, upgraded kitchen.

Koya, I said to myself, *you cannot afford this apartment. You can barely afford the studio! What are you thinking?* But I was so in love, and oh my god, I wanted it. I decided to do it. I was confident that I'd figure out how to make an extra few hundred dollars a month and make it work.

Moving into that apartment was the best decision I ever made. Taking on a little more in rent, stretching myself just a little bit, pushed me to grow in new and wonderful ways. It wasn't easy. I nicknamed the massage table I bought from Costco my "rent table," as the massages I started giving in my home helped to pay my bills. But that upgraded kitchen is where I started selling Koya's Kuisine, raw vegan food based on my own recipes, and teaching vegan cooking classes out of my home. I got my kitchen certified and started selling meals out of my home. I threw themed dinner parties each month—Revelations of Love, Revelations of Hope, Revelations of Forgiveness—where old friends and new ones would pay for a five-course raw vegan meal. It was like hosting a big Thanksgiving dinner every month—where I made all of the food! The five years that I lived in that apartment were a busy, beautiful time. But I still had my eye on an apartment with an ocean view.

Visiting a friend's apartment with a stunning vista refocused my intention to pursue one of my own. I started visualizing that ocean view every day. I thought about how beautiful it would be to wake up each morning and see the waves. It started to work. My dinner parties got more popular, and the people who attended connected me with bigger coaching clients. My social media started to blow up. Everything started to grow, and soon I was able to afford the apartment of my dreams.

Had I stayed in that small rented room or even that studio apartment, I wouldn't have been able to give massages, or start my catering business, or throw my dinner parties. I wouldn't be living where I am today, and more importantly, I wouldn't be the person I am today.

Stretch yourself and think a little bigger. When life presents you with an opportunity to grow, take it. It's so easy to stay small. I wanted to stay small. I wanted that little studio because I thought it was as much as I could get. And sure, I could believe that housing specialist was trying to upsell me—and he was—but he also pushed me to test my limits and in the end it helped me grow. It was a good deal on an apartment of that size and location. Making that one choice helped me to grow and expand in ways that have tremendously impacted my whole life.

Do the things that scare you most.

Now, I'm not saying you should go into deep debt or be irresponsible, especially with your finances, but sometimes you can push yourself a little bit further than you thought. Going even just a little bit outside of your comfort zone can make you stronger.

It might tire you out. It might stress you out. But you will get stronger.

Think big. Dream juicy. Stretch further. Don't miss out on the beautiful growth opportunities that are just waiting for you.

Think about your ideal reality. Are you stretching yourself as far as you can go? How could you stretch yourself a little bit more? What would that look like?

Do the Work

Manifesting your ideal reality takes some work. You can't just visualize what you want to achieve and expect it to come. You can't just think it; you have to feel it. And in order to feel it, you have to do your research. The more time you spend learning about what you want and getting clear on what really excites you about it, the more likely you are to attract it.

For example, perhaps you want to own a home. Okay, well, what does that involve? Do you know the process for purchasing a home? Have you spoken with other homeowners about what it's like to own property? Have you visited a variety of homes to find out what you do and don't like about them?

Or maybe you want a new relationship. You have to get out there and start dating! One of my clients thought all she needed to do was imagine the man of her dreams and voilà! He'd appear at her front door with a big smile and a bouquet of roses. Let me tell you, it doesn't happen that way. You have to find out what kind of person you are attracted to as well as who you're not attracted to. A lot of times, the type of person we think we want to be in a relationship with isn't the right fit after all. You think you want to be with an accomplished business owner, but then he's always working, and you need more quality couple time to be happy. How else would you know that unless you dated a bunch of guys? Put on your dating shoes and meet a variety of people in all kinds of situations. Figure out what type of personalities and physical qualities really align with yours. That's you doing your research. This way, when you visualize the man you want to manifest, you can describe him in detail. You know what he looks like, what being with him feels like, and how he makes you feel. Then he has a much better chance of showing up in your life.

Or maybe your ideal reality involves a lot of travel. Well, where? Do you want to travel in the U.S.? Internationally? With purpose? On vacation? On a mission trip? With whom do you want to travel? To manifest my trip to Morocco, I let the universe know of my desire—and then I got to work! I reached out to folks for advice and possible ways to make the trip happen. I let my community know I was interested in checking out eco-friendly hotels in Morocco for a possible destination yoga retreat. I investigated the cost of a plane ticket and identified the points of interest I wanted to visit and the experiences I wanted to have (exotic gardens, please!). And then, a few weeks later, someone who was helping me with research called with the words, "You're all booked!" An amazing resort had offered to host me for a few days in less than a month, and she'd gone ahead and finalized the plans. What else could I say but yes? I dropped everything and secured my flight. I believe that things that are meant to be will be, but I know they don't just happen. You can't just wait for what you want to fall into your lap. You need to be invested and 100 percent committed.

If you want to run a marathon, you have to get out there and run! You cannot visualize yourself to better physical fitness, no matter how much you wish otherwise! Visualization can help *improve* your performance. It helped me jump higher, run faster, and throw farther. But I was out on that track every day for four to six hours training, putting in the sweat, not sitting on the couch. When I use visualization today to improve my yoga practice or try a new acroyoga pose, I am also on the mat, giving it the effort of my heart and soul. Visualization alone isn't going to get you to the finish line unless you do the work to know the precise details of your ideal reality.

CREATING A VISION LIST OR VISION BOARD

Creating a vision list is a powerful tool to attract your dreams, your goals, and your ideal life. It will help you remember what really matters to you and make decisions that align with what's important to you. Review the list below. What speaks to you as something you'd like to manifest? Fill in the blank(s) to get you started.

My ideal career is _____

_____

My ideal partner is _____

_____

My ideal living situation is _____

_____

My ideal vacation is _____

_____

My ideal mood is_____

_____

I suggest keeping your vision list as short as possible. I've learned that when I focus my energy, things manifest more easily and powerfully in my life. It's okay if you have a long list . . . but remember, each item takes a little bit of your energy, and you only have so much. Do you want to spread it around or concentrate it? Lessening the energy you devote to an item means it may take a little bit more time and be more challenging to manifest.

Take a few moments to look at your vision list each day. I keep mine on my phone so I have it with me at all times. Visualize yourself having or experiencing what is on your list, and start bringing that energy into your life. (Use the step-by-step visualization practice on page 138 to help you.)

If you are a more visual person, create a vision board instead. Identify the emotion, experience, person, and/or object you wish to attract. (Again, I encourage you to concentrate on just one or two so that you can focus your energy.) Each goal should have its own vision board. You want your vision board to be as targeted and specific as possible. It shouldn't be cluttered—you don't want to bring more clutter and chaos into your life! Be particular about what you include. Make sure the photos, cutouts from magazines, drawings, words, and quotes you choose represent what you are trying to bring into your life. Less is more here.

For example, if you want to attract more joy, look for images that make you *feel* cheerful and upbeat. Don't get hung up on what the image is exactly but focus on how it makes you feel. Maybe a cute photo of playful puppies, two friends laughing together, or a gorgeous sunset inspires you. Add words (like "joy," obviously!) and quotes that describe how you want to feel. There are no limits to what can be on your vision board.

Reflect on your vision board each day. Keep it in a place where you'll see it regularly, such as on your nightstand or desk, or make a vision board using an online app and look at it on your phone or tablet. Take the time to consistently imagine what is on your vision board as real and present in your life so that you'll be more likely to attract it. (Use the following step-by-step visualization practice to help you.)

Visualization

Use this visualization to help you manifest the item(s) on your vision list or board. This example is for manifesting an experience—such as passing a certification test, hiking a mountain, graduating from college, or finishing a marathon. But by tweaking each step a bit, you can adapt it to apply to manifesting an object, person, or emotion. For the most powerful practice, before you begin, I suggest checking in with your chakras and making sure you're balanced.

- Clear your mind with a 5- to 10-minute meditation.

- Visualize the most optimal situation for your goal, with you as the star shining brightly and confidently. Don't leave your body in visualization. Stay in it.

- Let colors, sounds, and smells invade your senses. Feel the experience you desire to have in your body as if it's really happening. Don't just think and see it. Smell and feel it.

- See adversity. I know this might sound weird, but things don't always run smoothly. Visualize your greatest fear happening, and see yourself pushing past it.

- Write it all down. Now that you've seen your greatest self shine, describe it in words. Be confident that it will happen.

Back to Stardust

The practice of nonattachment goes hand-in-hand with visualization. We practice nonattachment so that we're not stuck on getting exactly what we want. We recognize an ideal outcome but know that if we shoot for the stars, we're going to land somewhere in the galaxy. We know the universe knows what we need and that sometimes what we need and what we want doesn't align. The reality you've visualized—the car, home, vacation, partner, job—may not appear exactly as you think it should. In that moment, you must trust the universe. In those times, I ask the universe, "If not that, then what?" This mantra keeps me optimistic and confident that what's meant for me will come to me and what's not meant will fall away. This helps me practice nonattachment and letting go while still being open to receive.

It's easy to become attached to things and people. Remember, we are spiritual beings having a human experience. Once we are done, we are going to keep the lessons that we learned during this life, but we're not going to keep our bodies or cars or homes. Those things are not lasting. Don't attach to them. We will all go back to stardust. Practicing nonattachment will help you move through life and move through loss a lot easier.

Recently, I lost my favorite wallet. I loved that wallet. It went with everything and was made of gorgeous, caramel-colored vegan leather. Perfect. As soon as I realized I'd lost it, I started beating myself up: *It's just like you to lose something so valuable and so beautiful.* Then I realized, *I can cancel all of my credit cards. I can replace my driver's license. I'll be absolutely fine.*

My intuition told me I must have just misplaced it somewhere, so I decided to wait and see if it would turn up. I checked the most likely places it would be in my home, but it wasn't in any of them. In every meditation, I invited my wallet back into my life. I went through each day as if at any moment my wallet was going to pop up and visualized how excited I would feel when it did. One morning, I opened a random drawer, and there it was. I must have tossed it in as I was rushing around to get ready for a party. I fell to the floor in relief. I laughed. I almost cried. These emotions felt amazing because I realized I had maintained peace of mind during the process. In yoga and meditation, I practice finding this place when things around me are in chaos. Practicing nonattachment while visualizing my ideal outcome has helped me through many difficult moments. I don't always end up finding the wallet, so to speak, but I have always found peace of mind and the ability to be more patient with myself.

You can't take a wallet, or any object, with you forever. Don't beat yourself up about losing it.

It's taken a while for me to accept this. I didn't have much growing up. I was raised on powdered milk and the Salvation Army. When I did get something, I was extremely grateful for it. I treated my first nice watch like it was the Holy Grail, it was so precious to me. Growing up this way taught me to appreciate things, but I also became a little too attached to them.

After my back injury, I started biking to help get my mind off not being on the field. I went all out on a new bike, a $3000 Cannondale racing bike with clip on shoes and all. I knew how valuable it was would motivate me to use it every day. And it did. I loved that bike and the way cycling made me feel. I joined biking teams. I got the biking outfit, the shoes, the whole kit and caboodle. Then one day I left the library and my lock had been cut. My bike was gone.

I was devastated. I cried and cursed. *Why me?* I felt so personally violated. I was in a bad mood and upset for days, telling everyone about how my bike had been stolen. It broke my heart that I'd spent so much money on that bike and someone just took it. Getting some insurance money to replace it made me feel a little better, but not much. Losing that bike made me feel sad for weeks. Then I remembered the bike was the reason I'd met my best friend, Nate the Great. One day when the chain fell off and I needed to get it fixed, Nate had walked with me for miles to the bike shop. We talked the whole way and really connected. In that moment, I realized that the bike was gone but the relationship it fostered remained. Once I switched my mind-set to one of gratitude, I wasn't sad anymore. Nate and I are best friends to this day.

Practicing nonattachment, or any other practice, isn't going to make you a different person overnight. What I've learned is that I'm not perfect. If someone takes something from me, I will get upset. But now I'm able to shift my emotions from anger and regret to compassion and gratitude a lot quicker. With continued practice, my funk that used to last a few weeks started to last only a few days, and now, almost instantly, I'm able to shift my attitude. Instead of thinking, *Oh, poor me*, and feeling terrible, I shift my attitude to compassion. *I hope this object blesses their life in the same way it blessed mine. I hope they really needed it. I hope they are in a better place in life because of it.*

Nonattachment and compassion put me into oneness, helping me to realize that nothing is really ours anyway. Everything belongs to the universe and, therefore, belongs to all of us. So if something leaves my possession, then it was meant to leave my possession. I shouldn't be attached to it. I should hope that it finds another home where it is needed. Practicing nonattachment keeps you in a place of peace and your heart full of love.

Nonattachment is particularly helpful if you are healing from a breakup, especially if you didn't end the relationship. If you're like me, you're crying and heartbroken, thinking, *How could they be so heartless? How could they say such mean things about me? How could they betray me like that?* But take a breath. Take a step back. Did you speak up about things that frustrated you in the relationship? Were you looking for more? If so, why not be grateful the relationship ended when it did? Its ending might be opening you up for something new, something better, and something more in alignment with your vibration. When one door closes, another door opens. But if we're so focused on looking at the closed door, we fail to see the new door opening.

Loss opens you up
to receive.

Uncommon Gains

Who or what are you attached to? List one thing:

_____

What are three qualities that you love about this person or physical item?

1. _____

2. _____

3. _____

Think about how those qualities make you feel. Are you able to feel those feelings without this person or thing?

Look around you. Does this person make you feel supported? Are there other people who are supportive? Does this object make you feel special? Are there other experiences that make you feel special? Most of the time, you have other sources for these feelings, but you've become focused on this one source making you feel a certain way. Recognizing that you are not dependent on just one source for these positive feelings will help you to practice nonattachment.

meditation practice

Follow the numbered meditation instructions on pages 14–15 and use the following as your intention:

I can see all of my needs being met as I flow through my days with ease and grace. I am getting closer to my dreams as I realize my true power is within. Every day I see love expressing as me.

Remember: Happiness Is an Inside Job

There is only one common denominator in your life: you. Your life will be filled with a variety of people, places, and experiences, but you are the one and only constant. The happiness attached to having other people or physical objects in your life—while wonderful—is temporary. The happiness that comes from inner peace, strength, and love is eternal. It takes practice, but the more you can find inner peace regardless of external circumstances, the more happiness you'll feel within. Each day, create space to play, laugh, and smile to cultivate your inner joy. It's nice to attract the things you want in life, but when happiness is chained to external gains, you can feel like a prisoner trapped in a certain situation. Go within. Breathe deep. Visualize your ideal reality while practicing non-attachment to free yourself.

affirmation practice

Say this affirmation several times upon waking in the morning and before going to bed at night:

I am free to express myself mentally, spiritually, and physically.

CHAPTER NINE

There Is Freedom in Discipline

Doing whatever you want to do, whenever you want to do it, with whomever you choose. No schedule, no commitments, just going where the day takes you. If you want to watch the news, you watch the news. If you want to use social media, you use social media. If you want to do yoga, you do yoga. Does that sound like freedom to you?

I've lived that life, and—as free as it might feel—it's not freedom. Sure, I could do whatever I wanted, but without a schedule or discipline, I ended up aimlessly running around all over the place, being late or altogether missing meetings, classes, and other opportunities that would have enriched me. I lost friends because I was living by the hour. I didn't make time for real conversations, meditation, or vacation. I was completely out of balance.

True freedom is based in love and aligns with your highest and greatest self. It supports self-care and self-love, enabling you to nurture yourself. Discipline helps you to attain true freedom. False freedom is based in fear and takes you away from the best version of yourself. It damages your body, mind, and soul. Is your freedom based in fear or based in love?

THE FREEDOM TO LIVE IN HARMONY

To live with your mind, body, and soul in harmony you need to consciously plan time to care for your mental, physical, and spiritual health. It's not going to happen by itself; you need to make it happen. If you meditate all day but never work out or socialize, you might be spiritually evolved, but you won't have the physical strength or social network to share your insights with the world. If you work out all day in the gym and never take the time to slow down, meditate, or recover, you might have nice muscles but your body will be inflamed and acidic because of no rest and regeneration time.

The discipline of a schedule gives you the freedom to live in harmony. When you follow a schedule, you make time for all of the important things in your life—including other people. We're not alone in this world. We co-habitate and co-create with other people every day. Discipline helps us respect our needs as well as the needs and time of others.

Schedule Everything

Put everything on your calendar, from the lime water you will drink in the morning to the time you will spend on doing your nails. When you put every activity into a schedule, you will be able to see how you are spending your time, *and* if you are spending too much time in any one area. (Make sure you are getting at least six hours of sleep!) A schedule will also help you to achieve your goals by presenting a clear vision of what you want to accomplish so your brain can get started on making what you want come true. Here's one of my daily schedules:

- 6 A.M.: Wake
- 6 A.M. to 8 A.M.: Morning routine
- 8 A.M. to 12 P.M.: Start workday
- 12 P.M. to 2 P.M.: Afternoon routine
- 2 P.M. to 6 P.M.: Evening sessions

- 6 P.M. to 8 P.M.: Dinner
- 8 P.M. to 10 P.M.: Passion projects, social time
- 10 P.M.: Night routine
- 10 P.M. to 6 A.M.: Sleep

When you schedule, you create more harmony in your life.

THE FREEDOM TO BE IN ALIGNMENT

Freedom is living in alignment with your highest self and being able to do what your heart and soul are telling you to do. To do so, you must have the time and space to listen to your inner voice. When you are confident about what you want and how you want to show up for your day, you can face the outside world and not be swayed by what others want for you. You can be guided by your inner voice and not controlled by the voices of others or the siren song of instant gratification. You can respond from a place of inner strength and intention.

You may want to eat cookies every day, and yes, you do have the freedom to do so. But is eating cookies every day in alignment with the body and the health that you want? Does it make you feel the way you want to feel? Eventually you're going to get a tummy ache, and I know that's not serving your greatest good.

My morning routine helps me to set a strong positive vibration at the beginning of each day. It's so important to set my day up right. My ideal morning looks like this:

- Wake up
- Write my morning pages
- Say my affirmations
- Meditate for 20 minutes
- Say my gratitude prayer
- Look at the water, look at the horizon during sunrise
- Drink 16 ounces of lime water with a pinch of cayenne pepper

- Do yoga for 30 minutes, usually beginning with Sun Salutations A and B

- Visualize my ideal day

- Walk or run one mile

- Take a cool shower

- Eat breakfast of a superfood smoothie or juice or a fruit plate with three to five of my favorite fruits

Only after breakfast will I post to social media, engage with friends, do work, or reply to e-mails. I feel empowered when I start my day this way, but let me be honest: sometimes I wake up and go straight to social media because there's something I want to say or a message I need to send. When I do that and go down the rabbit hole of socializing first thing in the morning, I feel a difference. My energy level is lower than when I follow my usual routine, staying in my own zone and in alignment with my own personal thoughts for the first few hours of my day.

When you start the day with social media, e-mail, or work, you align yourself with an external vibration. One friend starts his day with news because he likes to know what's going on in the world. Is this you? Or is social media your vice, like me?

Instead, begin your day in a positive vibration, aligned with you. Focus on yourself, your goals, and the good you're doing in the world. You don't always have to start your day alone, though; a few times a week, a friend joins me for my run. Whether I'm alone or with a partner, having the discipline to maintain time in the morning for reflection and alignment gives me the freedom to be my highest self.

I make time to check in with myself throughout the day as well. In the middle of each day, around lunchtime, I take a breather and connect with nature. I go outside, feel the sunlight on my skin, and take a deep inhale. Doing so helps me process stress, gives me a dose of vitamin D, and wipes the slate clean for the afternoon. Taking an extra breath if I've had a rough, tough, grouchy, rushed morning resets me for a different experience for the rest of the day. Small moments like these throughout the day keep me balanced and focused, but I know how easy it is to skip them (just one more e-mail!), so I made it a priority to put reminders on my calendar. Now, when I even think lunch, it's second nature for me to head out the door for some fresh air. It happens naturally, and I miss it, really miss it, if I skip a day. Establish some discipline around "small" moments throughout your day, and feel the large impact they can have on keeping you in alignment from dawn to dusk.

Create Your Own Morning Routine

Connecting with your breath, body, and soul in the morning cultivates an inner strength you can take with you throughout your day. Are there any practices from my morning routine that could become part of your own morning ritual? Are there others you'd like to include instead? Start with two to three practices or a routine of about 20 minutes and expand from there.

I hope you decide to include yoga as part of your ritual. A morning yoga routine is so special because the energy you cultivate at the start of your day sets the tone for the rest of it. See my website (koyawebb.com) for the series of poses in Sun Salutations A and B and the Get Loved Up Yoga Flow.

It takes 21 days to create a habit, so for the next 21 days, make a commitment to your morning routine.

DISCIPLINE IS NOT PUNISHMENT

When we think of discipline, we usually think of punishment, like "no TV privileges because you missed curfew," or rules that stop us from doing something we want to do, like "no TV after 10 P.M." This sense of discipline as something restrictive and limiting is usually shaped when we're children. It's only much later, when we're adults, that we realize our parents used discipline to help make us better people. I'm not talking about physical or emotional abuse; those are inexcusable. And sometimes our parents got it wrong. But in general, I think parents discipline their children because they want what's best for them.

This is healthy discipline, rules and structures as a positive means to achieve your highest and greatest good. Learning healthy discipline is a form of self-care, a conscious, consistent focus on doing what is going to be the best for you in the long run. Here are a few examples:

- I'm going to spend 30 minutes each day developing the skills I need to achieve one of my goals (find a new job, apply for a new certification, volunteer in my community).

- I'm going to cut out sugar because I know it's not good for me.

- I'm going to make a weekly schedule so I allocate enough time to my mental, spiritual, and physical health.

- I'm going to commit to a morning routine.

Unhealthy discipline, on the other hand, is extreme and hurtful. Examples of this might include:

- I'm going to focus only on instant gratification.

- I'm going to starve myself for a year.

- I'm not going to see friends until I achieve my ideal body.

- I'm going to get a jump on work by doing an extra hour of e-mails as soon as I get up in the morning.

Consistency of uplifting habits is what keeps dreams alive. Consistent work, creativity, and practice will help you stay in alignment with your desires. Where can you add more consistency or discipline in your life? Make a commitment to yourself to be more disciplined in this area. And yes, schedule a consistent time for it.

And don't forget to be disciplined about making time for play! You thought play was just for kids? Playing with your romantic partner, co-workers, pets, friends, and children will improve your mood, relieve stress, and fire up your creativity. Schedule some active playtime daily.

What are some ways to play? Well, what did you have fun doing as a child? Playing tag or hide-and-seek? Pillow fights? Skipping rope? Shooting hoops? Tossing a ball with your dog? Throwing a Frisbee with a friend? Save the board games for relaxation time. We want to be moving around during playtime. Have fun and laugh often! Playing is a time to step away from the adult world of responsibilities, disconnect from your everyday routine, and reconnect with your inner child.

It takes discipline to allocate time for play each day, but the rewards are worth it.

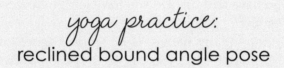

yoga practice:
reclined bound angle pose

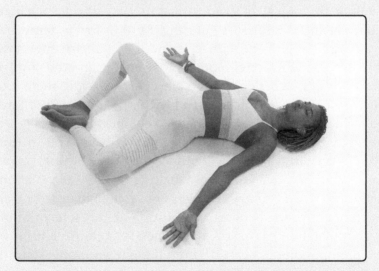

- Lie on your back.
- With an exhale, bring the soles of your feet to touch each other, and draw them toward your pelvis.
- Release your knees toward the floor.

151

- Bring your arms several inches away from your torso, palms facing up.
- Close your eyes.
- Find stillness.
- Hold the pose and take slow, deep breaths.
- Supporting your knees with your hands, straighten your legs with an exhale.

USE FAITH TO FACE FEARS

What do you have faith in? Do you have faith in love, or do you have faith in fear?

Love goes by many names: God, Spirit, Higher Power, the Universe. No matter what you call it, it is the positive energy that flows through all of us and unites us. Love vibrates at a high frequency and is all that is uplifting. Faith in love is faith that if you are in alignment with love and living at that high love vibration, you will attract more positive energy and the positive people, things, experiences, and emotions vibrating there too. When you are in alignment with love, in the vibration of love, you have faith that you will be able to conquer your fears.

Fear vibrates at a low frequency. If you have faith in fear, if you believe in fear, you will attract the people, things, experiences, and negative emotions vibrating in the fear vibration. Doubt, worry, and competitiveness are in alignment with fear. Yes, competitiveness. A focus on beating or besting someone lowers your vibration. Have you ever beaten someone in a game or for a promotion or prize, and—even though you won—you still didn't feel good inside? That's because you focused on winning and not on being your best. Be your best, and it won't matter who "wins." You've won already. Fear takes us away from being our best selves, and a faith in fear prevents you from becoming who you are meant to be.

The energy that you have faith in will determine what type of energy you receive. The energy that you put your faith in is the energy that will shape your reality. If you have faith that you're going to excel, to grow up to be a doctor, for example, and you put all of your heart and soul into studying and achieving that dream, then it's more than likely you will achieve it. If you have fears and tell yourself self-defeating things such as *I'll never be smart enough or good enough; I'll never get the help I need*, you're putting your faith in those fears, and it will be more than likely you're not going to do it.

This applies to *everything*.

So where are you putting your faith? In fear or in love?

CHOOSE TO BELIEVE

Faith is belief in something that you can't see or touch. It challenges you to believe even when you're thinking *I don't believe this yet* or wondering *How can I believe without proof?* Faith is *choosing* to believe despite these unknowns and unknowables.

Faith is a practice. Each and every day, ask yourself, *How can I practice my faith in love?* You might not see results for a long time, but choosing to believe, doing what's right for you, and putting your best foot forward will yield positive results.

When I moved to California, I was afraid that I wouldn't find a job or have enough money. But I didn't put my faith in those fears. Instead, I decided to trust my intuition and just go. I had faith that if I did my best to make a life for myself and stayed positive and confident, then something beautiful would happen. I had no proof that it was going to work, but my faith gave me the courage to overcome my fears. My life hasn't unfolded exactly as I'd planned, but it is better than I ever imagined because I keep expanding my faith.

Choose to believe in love, and take one step closer to achieving your soul's desire.

If you are struggling to have faith, identify where you feel doubt, and use your vision list or vision board and the visualization exercise on page 138 to help you feel what being without doubt would be like. Affirmations and meditation are other ways to bring you back to the vibration of love.

> *Believe in love. Believe you can attain your goals. And you will.*

meditation practice

Follow the numbered meditation instructions on pages 14–15 and use the following as your intention:

I am free to express myself mentally, spiritually, and physically. I release all negative thoughts about myself and others. I step into my next level of greatness with confidence and determination. I am grateful I allowed my challenges to make me stronger. I'm ready to graduate to nonattachment and true freedom.

RETURN TO LOVE

Faith in love means knowing that even when your life is falling apart, it won't stay that way. It will come back together. When you keep your faith in love even during the darkest times, you'll see that there will always be someone to help you. As long as you're reaching out, trying, putting forth the effort, someone is going to be in the positive vibration with you and help you out.

But it's not easy to hold fast to a faith in love. As we've seen, fears lurk everywhere. Limiting beliefs are especially easy to succumb to: *I'm not going to make it; I'm not going to make any friends; I'm never going to find love.* These thoughts can creep in at any moment, each day. You know how to transform limiting beliefs, but a strong faith in love provides a force field against them. Reinforce your faith in love, and those limiting beliefs won't even cross your mind. You've tapped into a higher vibration. But beware: when your faith in love is shaken, that force field weakens, and you can more easily fall into your fears and possibly get smothered by them.

One of the most common ways faith in love is shaken is when a dream doesn't materialize as quickly as hoped or in the way you had hoped. Faith plays the long game, and that can be difficult to take. The process of publishing this book shook my faith. I was so excited to write and share my ideas, but I had no idea of the process it takes. It took me over a year to finalize a deal. If I'd given up, if I'd lost my faith, you wouldn't be holding this book in your hands right now.

It's so easy to have your faith shaken when you stop listening to yourself and start listening to others. At the start of my publishing journey, I was in alignment with my soul—it was time. I was so excited to begin. And then one person started telling me what to do. And another person. "Are you sure you want to do that?" a friend asked. "Do you know what happened to me when I tried to do that?" said another. They shared their negative past experiences and all of their fears. They weren't trying to bring me down; their advice actually made a lot of sense. But as their voices crowded out my own, my faith was shaken. Trying to listen to everyone, I'd stopped listening to myself and started moving from love mode to fear mode, second-guessing myself. *Maybe I should rethink this. Maybe I should stick to what I know. Maybe I should move forward in a different way.*

Even at your most confident, you can be shaken by someone else's fears. At 12, I wasn't a very strong swimmer, but I went swimming with a friend in the deep end of the pool anyway. I knew I couldn't swim very well, but I didn't know she didn't know how to swim that well, either. So there we were in the deep end when she started going under, flailing her arms. When I paddled over to try to help her, she pulled me under. I was so scared! I thought, *She's trying to kill me.* I got away from her as fast as I could and clung to the edge of the pool, relieved when the lifeguard jumped in and pulled my friend to safety. This incident sticks with me as a reminder: There will always be someone who is more fearful than you. And their fear can pull you under. Even if they're not intentionally trying to drown you in their fears, it can still happen. And if they're already sinking in fear—watch out. Unless you get away from that negative energy and those toxic emotions, you'll sink, too.

If this happens to you, remember those fears aren't even yours; other people gave them to you. You didn't start with them. You fearlessly imagined an ideal reality for yourself, just as I did when I envisioned myself publishing a book. I had thought about what I wanted in life, dreamed my wildest dream, and was putting my energy toward achieving it—and then fear crept in like a thief in the night. It rattled me. I was shaken off my journey, and when that happened, my energy changed. Once your energy changes, your attraction changes, and you're no longer attracting your ideal reality.

Once I realized this, I turned within to figure things out. I stopped listening to what others were saying and started listening again to what my soul and my heart were telling me. I meditated and practiced my affirmations regularly and used the power of visualization to get back in alignment with my truth and with love. I knocked those fears away with a baseball bat and felt renewed and reinvigorated to pursue my dream and the ideal future I'd created for myself—no matter what might happen. If that resulted in a book, wonderful, and if not, then the experience would teach me whatever it is my soul needs to learn. And I have learned a lot. Publishing a book is an experience I am grateful to have had, especially as I know how easily I could have missed out on it.

When your faith is shaken or you feel yourself slipping into fear, return to your meditation; return to your affirmations. Return to everything you now know about how to challenge fear, and listen to what your heart and soul are calling you to do. Return to your true desire, and return to love. Your fears will go away.

*Don't let anyone's darkness
dim your light.*

CELEBRATE THE JOURNEY

Living your best life and becoming your best self is a journey. Enjoy it! Pause and celebrate each milestone, no matter how "small" or seemingly insignificant, along the way. Celebrating is a way of acknowledging how you're changing as you grow more in alignment with your soul's desire and your ideal reality. Celebrating builds confidence and momentum, and it puts you in a state of gratitude and raises your vibration.

While it is satisfying to check off a goal as accomplished and call it a day, celebrating the realization of a goal maximizes the satisfaction by deepening its meaning. Instead of mindlessly progressing from one goal to the next, take the time to mindfully recognize the progress you are making.

Don't wait for the "big win" to celebrate. We all tend to focus on big goals—finishing a degree, landing a new job, buying a new home, starting a new business, running a 10K—and forget to acknowledge how important all of the "little" steps are that get us there. Completing a class, updating your resume, investigating mortgages, drafting a business plan, and running one mile are essential milestones on your journey. I was raised to be humble, so my default is to think, *You know, that's no big deal.* But these accomplishments are a big deal. Without them, your journey can be stressful and hard. Celebrate the milestones and the journey.

My goal to release a music single involved many steps along the way. First I had to write the song, then record it. Next, I had to create the music video and, finally, put the song and video out there for the world to hear and see. At each step, I pushed past my fears. And that's worth celebrating. Every time you push past a fear, every time you choose love, celebrate. We should have something to celebrate every single day.

Mark Your Progress

Take a moment to redo the inventory on page 16. Has anything changed since you've started doing some of the practices in this book? Acknowledge the positive ways your life is changing.

On a scale of 1 to 10, with 10 being the most positive, think about how you would rate these parts of your life:

Health　　　　1　2　3　4　5　6　7　8　9　10

Relationships　1　2　3　4　5　6　7　8　9　10

Career　　　　1　2　3　4　5　6　7　8　9　10

Spirituality　　1　2　3　4　5　6　7　8　9　10

Each week, set aside some time to chronicle and reflect on your growth. Use the following prompts to identify where you've grown during the week and where you see opportunities for more growth. Focus on one of these areas in the coming week.

How I grew: _____

_____

Areas where I was challenged: _____

_____

Areas that pose opportunities for growth: _____

_____

Treat Yourself

Celebrating is a form of self-care. Give yourself small rewards for a job well done with things or experiences that you already know you need, such as free time. Or treat yourself to something special. I like to go for a massage or to the spa as a beautiful way to practice self-care. A few months ago, I wanted to improve my website, and I told myself that if I worked on it for one hour each day for a week, I could have a "Works" Burger, my favorite vegan sandwich, from the Golden Mean Café in Santa Monica. Giving myself little treats like that kept me focused and motivated.

Each step on your journey matters. Each step closer to living your purpose should be celebrated. Affirm the progress you make and the successes you have each day. Did you choose love over fear? Then celebrate it!

Make a list of five ways to treat yourself:

1. _____

_____

2. _____

_____

3. _____

_____

4. _____

_____

5. _____

_____

Feel the Love and Support

Share your accomplishments with family and friends, and celebrate together. Make dinner as a group each week. Go for a walk. Including your loved ones on your journey is a powerful way to stay on track. And remember to celebrate your loved ones' successes as well.

Social media provides me a wonderfully supportive community. I know it's not for everybody, and a lot of people look at social media as a waste of time that disconnects us from the people in our "real" life. But it's been a positive for me. Connecting this way has helped me establish a vibrant social network of friends and family all over the world, from Bali to Jamaica to Hawaii. How amazing is it to celebrate with such a diverse community? Having friends, family, or a community nearby to celebrate with in person is profound, but celebrating with people who live thousands of miles away and have very different backgrounds yet still share your values is so beautiful.

When I first started doing yoga, posting on social media every day helped me keep my practice consistent. I'm not sure I would have stuck with it if not for the flood of encouragement and support that came through the internet. In turn, I inspired others by posting consistently. Now my network helps keep me accountable and sends good wishes when I meet any of my goals. Each day, after I run or walk my mile, I post a photo on Instagram. I love reading the supportive messages people send in response and watching as others complete their own walk or run for the day and send a snap of themselves. Together, we're pressing through our fears.

Using social media can make it easy to forget something very important, though: everything you're looking for can be found within. Don't let your happiness and sense of self-worth depend on other people's approval and validation. If social media isn't helping you to grow or build a supportive community, inspiring you in some way, or raising your vibration, make some changes in how you use it so that it can be a positive force in your life.

Or step away and turn within. Is how you're using social media aligning with your soul's purpose?

Most people either really like social media or really don't. It's a personal thing. I love it, but if you don't or you don't have a natural interest in it, don't use it. Focus on rewarding yourself and celebrating with your loved ones. Focus on the family- and community-building activities that speak to you.

Remember: Move Forward Unafraid

When you are in alignment with who you want to be, you move through your day mindful of the practices that help you to live your best life. Discipline will come naturally, intuitively. Until then, remember there is freedom in discipline, and make a conscious choice to use healthy discipline as a way of attaining the freedom to achieve your greatest good and be your best self.

Let your faith in love conquer any fears you have about moving forward with your soul's desire. Don't worry about how it will happen. Often the most beautiful things in life make no sense in the beginning. Just close your eyes every day, breathe deep, and trust your intuition to guide you. Your path does not have to be perfect in anyone else's eyes for it to be blessed. Practice meditation and go within to work out things that don't make sense. Trust your soul, and trust the path of love to bring you where you want to go.

Give love. Inspire others to find strength and confidence. There are so many people who need more love and less fear in their lives. Show the people around you that you love and support them.

affirmation practice

Say this affirmation several times upon waking in the morning and before going to bed at night:

I am divinely supported and provided for.

CHAPTER TEN

You Are Unstoppable

You're listening to your heart, and you know what you want. You've visualized your ideal reality and are taking steps to manifest it. You may be passionate about making a lot of changes in your life. In fact, I hope you are! That's exciting, but it can also be overwhelming. You need to have clarity and focus now more than ever. You can't do everything all at once; trying to do so will only frustrate you. You won't make good progress in any one area, and I guarantee you'll get discouraged. Or, with so many options to choose from, you may stall and get stuck from overwhelm.

Have you heard the popular "rocks, pebbles, sand in a jar" analogy? Fill a large, empty jar with rocks, and it looks full, right? Add a handful of pebbles, give the jar a shake so they spread out among the larger rocks, and the jar still looks full. Then, pour sand into the jar to fill up all of the remaining empty space. Now the jar is completely full.

The jar represents your life. The rocks are your most important projects and goals. If you only had those rocks in your jar, your life would feel full and complete.

The pebbles represent the things in your life that matter but that you could live without. The sand represents all of the other little things that tend to help you waste time, complaining about things you don't have the guts to change or mindlessly scrolling through Instagram. If you fill your life up with too many pebbles and a lot of sand, you won't have any room for the big rocks. This is where clarity and focus come in—to help you identify your big rocks and prioritize them.

With *clarity*, you'll see the goals that matter most to you right now and the specific steps you'll take to achieve them. With *focus*, you'll know why you're so passionate about reaching your milestones and locate that extra wellspring of strength to tap into when adversity strikes. With clarity and focus, your energy is directed and powerful. You are in control, and soon you will be living the life of your dreams—and enjoying the journey.

GET CLARITY

Why do you think your soul is here? Right now, in this lifetime, what is your soul's purpose? In other words, what is your mission in life? Write it down here:

_____

_____

_____

_____

The answer to this question is your Mission Statement, and fulfilling this task should be your priority. It will bring you the highest level of happiness.

We are all born with something that makes us special. Some of us were lucky and connected directly with that magic when we were kids. By the time we're adults, we've already identified our gift and how best to share it. For others, our Mission Statement may take some time to figure it out. Never stop looking for your purpose in life or doubt that it exists. Do the work, and I assure you, you will find it. Start by checking in with your heart and soul. Go within through meditation and reflection. What activity brings you joy? What are you good at? Whether its painting, growing vegetables, or being around children, keep doing it and do more of it. Activities that you love, that cause time to zoom by when you do them, will lead you to your mission.

The most powerful is a mission that fulfills you *and* helps others. A mission is not selfish, like making money to buy more stuff. Remember, whatever you put out into the universe, the universe will bring it back to you in one way or another. Your mission will come from a place of abundance and selflessness.

I'm here to raise the love vibration of the planet. That's my Mission Statement. It's big and broad but powerful. Once you're clear on your mission, you can get clear on what you'll do to achieve it, step by step. First, ask *How?*

> *Question:* How will I raise the love vibration of the planet?
> *Answer:* Through education.

Then dig deeper and keep asking questions to drill down into your Mission Statement. This will lead to a specific, achievable goal. For example:

> *Question:* What type of education?
> *Answer:* Education focused on holistic health and healing.

> *Question:* What form will the education take?
> *Answer:* Online courses.

> *Question:* How will you create the online courses?
> *Answer:* I will write the scripts and partner with a videographer to shoot them.

And so on until you reach specific goals with measurable markers of successful completion. For example, writing the script for one episode of my video series is a manageable goal. Setting your goals in this way will help you attain your ultimate desire by crystallizing the vague ideas floating in your mind into small, discrete action steps. It ensures that you are channeling your time, energy, and efforts into things that really matter to you. And it makes you live more consciously.

Everything in this world is created twice, first in your mind and then in reality. Without mental creation, physical creation is tough. When you set a goal, you create it in your mind. You have set into motion a reality for yourself, and now the universe can help you materialize it in physical reality.

Set Your Goals

Now that you have your Mission Statement, what are some goals that will help you to achieve it? Remember to make your goals as specific and detailed as possible. For example, "help kids learn to read" is much too broad and overwhelming to easily track your progress. Instead, dig deeper and keep asking, *How?* Setting the goal to volunteer at your local library's literacy program is more specific.

Write your goals down, and keep them where you will see them often, such as on a notecard on your nightstand or on your smartphone. Then revisit your vision board or vision list. Has anything changed? Have there been any shifts that should be incorporated? Consider adding your Mission Statement.

What's Your "Why?"

Why have you identified the Mission Statement that you have? Maybe it just feels right to you, but take a moment to try to articulate exactly why it speaks to you so profoundly. Look at a goal you've identified in the previous practice. Why is fulfilling that goal important to you? Write it down. Putting your feelings onto paper crystallizes them in your mind and creates a focal point for your attention. This is how you get focused.

Mission Statement: _____

_____

Why: _____

_____

Goal 1: _____

_____

Why: _____

_____

Do you still want to pursue it? _____

_____

Goal 2: _____

_____

Why: _____

_____

Do you still want to pursue it?_____

_____

Goal 3: _____

_____

Why: _____

_____

Do you still want to pursue it?_____

_____

If you can't come up with a good why, or your why is not very meaningful, it's time to reevaluate your goal. For example:

Goal: To release a song.

Why: Because my friend did.

That why isn't going to help me raise the love vibration of the planet. If your why helps you get closer to your Mission Statement, keep the goal. If it doesn't, your energy is better spent on a different goal or finding a why that satisfies your soul. Look inward. Do the practices in this chapter again and find a clear, meaningful why.

It will help you a lot to have a clear why when you hit a roadblock. Reminding myself that I wanted to release a song to inspire others helped keep me going when I had trouble writing the song and was afraid to release it. My why gave me the strength to look that fear in the face and the confidence to be persistent no matter how many hurdles and roadblocks came my way. And there were several. But I was motivated to keep pushing for what I believe in—and you will be too.

Focus on One Goal

This practice really helps me to focus on a goal, especially if I've been procrastinating. Choose your top-priority goal. Write it down along with your Why on a large and noticeable piece of paper and put it under your pillow. Read them both after you wake up each morning and again before you go to sleep. Keep this paper under your pillow to remind you.

DODGE DISTRACTIONS

If you know what you want and have a clear set of goals for how to get it, but you aren't getting closer to achieving it, you probably have too many distractions. This is a common problem. Distractions are *everywhere*. You may not even recognize some of them, they're so much a part of life. It's easy to become bombarded with them. While you'll never get rid of them completely, you can be aware enough to navigate them and stay focused on what you need to do while handling the situations that randomly pop up and demand your attention. Distractions are not all the same. Some are healthy, and others are unhealthy. Healthy distractions include getting pregnant, buying a house, and attending a wedding, reunion, or funeral. Connecting with family and friends is healthy and good, but it can still distract you from your goal if you don't manage priorities. Unhealthy distractions are also abundant: too much partying, drinking, taking drugs, and spending too much time on activities, like gossiping, that do not help you achieve your goals. Yes, gossiping! It's a negative distraction, and it will suck your energy and joy if you engage in it too often, trust me.

Make a list of three healthy and three unhealthy distractions here or in your journal:

Healthy Distractions

1. _____

_____

2. _____

_____

3. _____

_____

Unhealthy Distractions

1. _____

_____

2. _____

_____

3. _____

_____

Healthy distractions are difficult because they are good things to have. Having friends and family means being present for them. Building a relationship or family takes time and attention. You need to go to your friend's wedding. You need to comfort your grieving cousin. You need to arrange for the roof of your house to be fixed. You need to care for your sick child. Having a life means having responsibilities.

If you are feeling overrun by healthy distractions, ask yourself, *What can I do to accomplish my goals in light of all of these responsibilities?* Maybe it's time to ask for help from friends or family to take some of the load off. Maybe a personal assistant or time-management tools would be useful.

Take a look at your list of healthy distractions. Acknowledge that these are a reality for you, and then consider, *What do I need to incorporate into my life to be on point to achieve my goals?* Brainstorm ideas, then make a commitment to do what you need to do to manage your healthy distractions better.

As for unhealthy distractions, you have to make a commitment to let them go. Limiting participation to once a month helps. For example, going out partying every few weeks could be okay for you. But be mindful of the impact on you and your progress. If you aren't achieving your goals, take another look at these activities. I had a big project I was trying to finish up, but my calendar was filled with social events that I really wanted to attend. Some simply promised to be a good time, but others involved supporting a friend or making valuable contacts. Spending so much time away from work was going to slow me down, but it didn't feel right to back out of everything, either. So I attended the events, saw who I needed to see, danced a little, ate a little, and showed my love a lot—then left early. I stayed for an hour, maybe two, and then went back home, re-energized to get to work. You don't have to throw your whole schedule off. Try allotting yourself two to four hours each day for play and social time—then get back to what you know is in alignment with what you are trying to accomplish.

This balance worked for me (I got the project done), but sometimes it's harder to mix the two. When I'm at home in California, I find it much harder to focus because I want to see all of my friends. It's a lot easier for me to go out at night and still stick with my schedule when I travel. In these cases, you may need to make a tough choice about how to spend your time and your energy. That's when you need to go within. Review your Mission Statement, goals, and your why. Do they still reflect the life you desire? If so, then recommit to that life each day and schedule your need to accomplish your goals each day. The more you affirm your purpose, the more you'll naturally avoid the unhealthy distractions that are preventing you from realizing it.

Yes, sometimes you just mess up and blow off what you know you should be doing. We're all human. I've done it more times than I'm proud of. Don't beat yourself up. Recognize these times as an opportunity for growth. Maybe your priorities have changed. Maybe fear is sneaking in and sabotaging you, and it's time to face it. Have compassion for yourself as you work to understand why you are behaving as you are, and commit to getting back in alignment.

The Pomodoro Technique

When I really want to knock something out, I use a system invented by entrepreneur Francesco Cirillo to focus my attention and minimize distraction. Known as the Pomodoro Technique, it breaks work down into short chunks of time called *pomodoros* after the tomato-shaped timer Cirillo used. I like to set about two to four hours aside for work and rest in 25-minute intervals. During the 25-minute breaks, I do yoga or call a friend. I've found I'm much more productive with focused work and play breaks.

SET YOUR BOUNDARIES

I'm a giver. I love to help people, and I often put other people's needs ahead of my own. A big heart and willingness to help others are two of my best qualities, but they can also make it difficult for me to stay on track to achieve my own goals. Assisting others can be a good thing, but if we take it too far, it can take us away from what we hope to accomplish.

Recently, I've been caring for my aunt. She unexpectedly wanted to extend her stay with me during a month when I planned to run a yoga teacher training in my home. I was already feeling pretty drained, making sure my aunt had everything she needed while maintaining a full schedule of work, but I didn't stress out. I recognized this as a healthy distraction and thought, *Well, I'll figure it out.* I wasn't going to cancel the training. It was too important to me and to the 12 women who'd signed up. Maybe I'd have to get another assistant to help with the training. But the most important thing I did was talk to my aunt and let her know what was happening and that I might not be as available to her during those few weeks. She appreciated knowing the situation and was completely understanding. What do you need to communicate to your loved ones so they can support you?

> *When you love yourself first, you can love others and the planet more.*

There was a time when I just kept quiet and soldiered on through all kinds of stressful situations without saying anything, but not anymore. When positive distractions have to do with family or close friends, I talk it out, clearly articulating my goals to them. Let's face it: people are needy by nature. But you can't expect people to be mind readers. They don't know what your goals are unless you tell them. So tell them! Share what your goals and commitments are, and ask for their aid and support to keep you on track. We all want to feel loved and supported.

Many people avoid family and friends when focusing on a goal, but you don't have to completely isolate yourself. Just set your boundaries—and honor them. It's okay to say "no" to more responsibilities. Most likely, like my aunt, your loved ones will support you and be there for you. If they aren't, well, then you'll know right away where you need to set your boundaries. It can be hard to distance yourself from a loved one, but if he or she is actively derailing your progress and preventing you from accomplishing your goals, you have to do so. Be intentional about with whom you share your light, and mindful about how you share your energy. It's limited: conserve it to spend on who and what truly matters to you. Surround yourself with people and mentors who are invested in your victory.

The Skill of Setting and Sustaining Boundaries

I admit: I have trouble setting boundaries. I put others ahead of myself all of the time. I lose sleep because I've said "yes" to way more things than I can handle. I know stretching myself thin like this isn't good for me, making me feel tired and depleted. Being generous and open-hearted with my time, possessions, and emotions is my nature, and it's tough to say "no." Practicing my daily wellness routine is one way I've found to keep me feeling strong, confident, energized, ready for anything the world has to offer me, and better able to set my boundaries.

How do you know when you are protecting yourself and when you are being selfish?

Setting and sustaining boundaries is a skill. Unfortunately, it's a skill that many of us don't learn. We might pick up pointers here and there from experience or through watching others, but for many of us, boundary-building is a relatively new and challenging concept. Here are my tips for setting boundaries:

- **Tune in to your feelings of discomfort and resentment.** Think of these on a scale from 1 to 10. If your ranking is at the higher end of this scale, ask yourself, *What is the cause?* Resentment usually comes from being taken advantage of or being unappreciated, and it's a good indication that you have to set limits.

- **Practice good communication skills.** Be clear and direct. Say "no" and mean it. There are people who will try to change your mind, guilt-trip you, or push you into doing something you have already decided that you do not want to do. Stand your ground. You need—yes, need—to take care of you.

- **Practice self-awareness.** Setting boundaries involves honing in on your feelings and honoring them. If you notice yourself slipping and feeling resentful, ask yourself, *What's changed?* Consider what you are doing that prevents you from keeping your boundaries. With those answers in mind, mull over your options, asking, *What am I going to do about the situation? What do I have control over?*

Setting boundaries takes courage and practice, but it's a skill you can master.

> *When distractions arise, remember your why, recommit, and use visualization to focus your energy.*

EAT RIGHT, MOVE REGULARLY, FEEL GREAT

Your body carries your soul and essence while you are on Earth. The better you treat it, the longer you will get to enjoy life to the fullest. Your body thrives on healthy food, regular exercise, and good sleep.

I feel so much better and full of energy when I eat food from the earth. A vegan plant-based diet supports my optimal health and the health of the planet. But I haven't been vegan all of my life; as an athlete from the South, I ate everything that was put in front of me. My mom cooked at home, so I didn't consume much processed food until I went to college, where I put the "freshman 15" to shame by gaining a whopping 25 pounds. I started to feel sluggish and experience digestive health issues because of the poor quality of food I was consuming. When I stopped eating processed food, my health improved dramatically, and I found adding more fruits and veggies to my diet made me feel even better. Now completely vegan, I experience heightened levels of energy, vitality, and clarity every day. It certainly wasn't an easy transition in the beginning, but enjoying a plant-based vegan diet was a conscious decision I made in my life 13 years ago, and I don't intend to ever go back. I encourage you to make good nutrition a priority, bring more plant-based foods into your diet, and reduce the amount of processed foods you consume. Use my 7-Day Meal Plan (page 193) as a jump start! Eating this way will boost your energy, improve your digestion, and minimize your risk of chronic disease.

Another tip: get your blood work done once a year to check for deficiencies in vitamins and minerals, such as iron, vitamin D, calcium, folate, and magnesium. Work with your doctor or health coach to find ways to correct any deficiencies with food or supplements.

Move your body every day. Ditch the excuses that you are too out of shape or not athletic. Walking a mile a day is a great way to begin if you haven't exercised in a while. There are so many fun ways to get your blood pumping. Find something you enjoy doing, such as turning up the music and dancing for 20 minutes straight! The important thing here is to get your body moving each and every day.

Sleep rejuvenates your mind and body and is as essential to your health as good nutrition and regular exercise. Each person requires a different amount of sleep to feel rested and refreshed upon waking, but aim for six to eight hours of actual sleep each night. If you have a hard time getting to sleep, wake frequently throughout the night, or wake feeling lethargic or mentally foggy, you may not be getting enough quality sleep. Improving your sleep hygiene habits can help dramatically. For me, following a consistent night routine and keeping a regular sleep schedule is essential.

So let's take care of your total body with some of my recommendations. I love to allocate one day each week, Sunday for example, to really focus on taking care of my total body, inside and out. I eat healthy food, get a massage, practice yoga, and meditate longer. Try it!

Drink a Smoothie a Day

A smoothie a day keeps the doctor away! A smoothie is the best way to mix vitamins, nutrients, and deliciousness in one glass. You can have one for breakfast or as a snack or meal replacement. The flavor options and ingredient combinations are truly endless. Experiment! Just be sure to use a mix of fruits, superfoods, and protein.

I like to drink a green smoothie in the morning for an extra kick of energy to start the day with a blast! Trust me, it's better for you than coffee in the long run.

Eat a Salad a Day

Having a salad for one meal each day is a great way to add more veggies to your diet. Plus, a salad for lunch won't make you tired if you have to get back to work, and one for dinner won't leave you feeling stuffed and heavy, so you can get a good night's sleep.

If you think salads are boring, think again. Start with a base of leafy greens. My favorite is kale. Then pick your five favorite vegetables (or mix it up with a combination of veggies and fruits), add some protein, such as lentils or nuts, and sprinkle on some seeds. Use a dressing that you love. Try ones made with citrus fruits, mustard, garlic, or fresh herbs. My favorite one is lemon avocado dressing. It's super simple: in a bowl, add the juice of a whole lemon, one avocado, a pinch of pink Himalayan sea salt, and a pinch of black pepper, and massage into your greens of choice. You will be amazed at how good it tastes with any kind of salad. The right dressing makes a big difference!

Still need some motivation to prepare a salad a day? If you use social media, set a goal to post a picture of your salad each day. To make your food look beautiful, you'll need to use a lot of colorful fruits and veggies, and I know for Instagram you'll make an extra effort to be creative and original with your ingredients, toppings, and dressings. A salad dressing tip: toss or massage (I like to get my hands dirty!) leafy greens with dressing before adding the other ingredients. You won't need to use much dressing—one avocado or two tablespoons of oil max—to coat each leaf and taste its flavor in every bite. Don't go overboard on dressing and end up with more calories that you planned for.

Hydrate

How much water do you drink in a day? Most of us don't drink nearly enough. On average, people tend to drink about 1.5 liters each day when we should be drinking around 3 liters per day. Your body consists mostly of water, so hydration is critical to keeping all of your systems running smoothly. Not drinking enough water can make you tired, give you a headache, or cause digestive troubles. Here are some tips for a more hydrated lifestyle:

- Set a large glass of water by the bed when you go to sleep and drink it first thing when you wake up in the morning. This is helpful for pulling out toxins from the previous day, and it refreshes your body, preparing it for the day ahead.

- Keep a bottle of water accessible throughout the day, whether you are on the go or sitting at a desk. Having water close by will remind you to take a sip regularly.

- Infuse your water: Add a few mint leaves, a wedge of lemon, a few slices of cucumber, or a twist of lime to water to liven it up and make it more tempting to sip often.

- Consume raw fruits and vegetables that are high in water content, such as watermelon, grapefruit, strawberries, star fruit, celery, tomatoes, spinach, and broccoli.

Practice Yoga

Yoga is a great way to improve your fitness and flexibility but it is more than just pretty poses. Many people don't know—until they experience it—that yoga is deeply and profoundly healing. It relieves stress, detoxifies, and strengthens us physically, mentally, and spiritually. I hope you've experienced these benefits for yourself. And, if you haven't yet, why not try the yoga practice in this chapter?

yoga practice:
upward-facing dog pose to
downward-facing dog pose

- Lie on your stomach with your forehead on the floor, palms beside your chest, and legs stretched back.
- Inhale, straighten your arms, lift your torso up, press the top of your feet into the floor, and lift your thighs. Hold for one breath.

- Exhale. Press through your hands, lift your hips up toward the sky, and press your heels down and back.

Clear Heavy Metals

Toxic heavy metals, such as mercury, aluminum, copper, cadmium, lead, arsenic, nickel, chrome, and steel, are everywhere in our environment, and they make their way into our bodies through the air we breathe, the food we eat, and the clothes we wear. They cause damage to our brains and bodies and have been linked to mood disorders, depression, and memory loss. Remove these destructive chemicals from your body by eating these detoxifying foods: cilantro, wild blueberries, spirulina, barley grass juice powder, and Atlantic dulse.

You can try eating these daily in a smoothie like my Heavy Metal Electric Detox Smoothie, aligned with the alkaline diet created by Dr. Sebi, a biochemist, herbalist, and healer. It is made up of live, raw foods (called "electric") that are alkaline, which means they control the acid levels in the body. According to Dr. Sebi's research, high acid levels in the body are linked to disease. The following smoothie is inspired by the Heavy Metal Detox Smoothie of Anthony Williams, the Medical Medium, and Dr. Sebi's alkaline diet.

HEAVY METAL ELECTRIC DETOX SMOOTHIE

2 Burro bananas
2 cups wild blueberries, frozen
1 cup cilantro
1 cup water
1 teaspoon barley grass juice powder
1 teaspoon spirulina
1 small handful of Atlantic dulse
Optional: water to blend

Run or Walk a Mile a Day

Running or walking a mile a day is part of my morning routine, and I hope you'll make it a part of yours. It brings tremendous health benefits, including all of the following:

- extends longevity
- prevents heart disease
- promotes good blood circulation
- reduces the risk of diabetes and cancer
- gives you a natural endorphin high!

Do I need to say more? Try it once, focus on how good you feel afterward, and make it a daily habit.

Do HIIT Workouts

HIIT, high-intensity interval training, got me in shape for track in college, and I've kept it as part of my weekly fitness routine ever since. I love how, in as little as ten minutes, these short, intense bursts of exercise followed by a brief recovery period can improve your fitness levels and overall health. A HIIT workout strengthens your body, speeds up your metabolism, and improves the health of your heart. Plus, you don't need equipment, and you can pretty much do it anywhere. Try a HIIT workout I created (there are many available on my website or Get Loved Up app) at least once a week. It's a nice enhancement to a regular yoga practice.

meditation practice

Follow the numbered meditation instructions on pages 14–15 and use the following as your intention:

I am divinely supported and provided for. I have everything that I need in life, and I use my thoughts, words, and actions to attract more love than I've ever imagined.

Massage

Massage provides so many benefits! It promotes relaxation, relieves anxiety, reduces muscle pain and tension, improves sleep, boosts your immune system, and eases headaches. Allow yourself some well-deserved massage "me time" each week.

Think a massage is too expensive? You don't need to go to the spa every week. A massage from your friend or partner, or even a self-massage, can make a huge difference.

Let's try it out: Take a deep inhale and exhale slowly. Where do you feel tightness in your body? Your shoulders, feet, back, or neck? Use your fingers and hands to apply gentle pressure and mindfully massage that area for a few moments. Increase the pressure, if you find it tolerable. How do you feel?

Be creative. There's always an opportunity to create magic.

Breathe

Breathing is something you just "do" automatically in order to survive, but you can breathe mindfully to help you cope with stress, increase your energy, and clear your mind. There are many different ways to breathe mindfully. Here are two of my favorites: Stimulating Breath, also called the Bellows Breath. Its aim is to raise vital energy and increase alertness. Try this exercise the next time you need an energy boost:

- Inhale and exhale rapidly through your nose, keeping your mouth closed but relaxed. Your breaths in and out should be equal in duration but as short as possible. This is a noisy breathing exercise.

- Try for three in-and-out breath cycles per second. This produces a quick movement of the diaphragm, suggesting a bellows.

- Breathe normally after each cycle.
- Do not breathe this way for more than 15 seconds on your first try.

Each time you practice the Stimulating Breath, you can increase your time by five seconds or so until you reach a full minute. If it's done properly, you should feel invigorated, with the same heightened awareness you feel after a good workout. You'll feel the effort in the back of the neck, the diaphragm, the chest, and the abdomen.

Breath of Fire is a great tool for invigorating your mind, boosting energy, and relieving anxiety. It also strengthens your core and cleanses your lungs.

- Sit in a comfortable position. Lengthen your spine.
- Rest your hands on your knees. Close your eyes. Inhale naturally.
- Forcefully exhale through your nose by actively drawing your belly toward your spine. Keep the rest of your body still. Inhale naturally.
- Repeat 10 rounds of this breath, exhaling forcefully and inhaling naturally at a medium pace. Then rest for a minute in Corpse Pose.

Avoid this exercise if you have high blood pressure. Stop immediately if you feel dizzy. Keep in mind that taking care of your body also means listening to it when it tells you what feels good and what doesn't and, above all, respecting it.

Remember: Be Love

People will often ask, "Who do you want to be?" or "What do you want to do with your life?" It's good to have an answer to those questions. It's empowering to have a goal and a set path for accomplishing it. But it's okay if you don't—you don't have to have everything all figured out. In fact, you don't ever have to figure anything out. You can "just" be an amazing person and that's enough.

It's easy to become preoccupied with determining the one job or role that defines who you are, especially if you take on many roles: artist, entrepreneur, mother, yogi. But our lives have many different seasons. Who we are constantly changes. Being overly concerned or focused on finding the thing that truly defines you leads to frustration, with judgment and depression following close behind. These emotions will only hold you back. Don't stress if you don't know who you want to be or what you want to do with your life. You can just live in the moment and be love.

CONCLUSION

You Got This

You have all of the knowledge and tools you need to connect to your inner confidence, overcome your fears, and achieve your dreams. If you do the work, and if you let your faith in love outweigh your faith in fear, you will be fierce and you will live your best life. If you feel weak, lost, or confused, go back to the practices in this book:

- Go back to meditation, and make sure you are aligned with what your soul wants you to do. Allow your highest self to lead you.
- Go back to your morning routine.
- Go back to your vision board.

You have everything you need to move forward with confidence.

This year, I used every tool in my toolbox to heal from trauma, process betrayal, restore my physical health, grow my business, forge supportive and meaningful relationships, release my first single, take my first international solo trip, and accomplish so many more of my personal and professional goals. There was a lot of joy and *a lot* of pain—at times, the most physical and emotional pain I've ever felt in my entire life. Through all of it, I was able to be strong and grow stronger. I can get through anything because I know how to use my challenges, setbacks, and fears as stepping-stones, not roadblocks. I know how to use them to help me walk the path of love and make me fierce. Now you do too.

No matter what you are going through or where you want to go, the practices I've shared in this book can help you too. Yoga, meditation, affirmations, visualizations, and the other tools and practices in this book amplify the voice of your authentic self, bust your limiting beliefs, and strengthen your connection to Spirit. They can transform your fears into opportunities for growth.

The most common FEAR acronym is:

Forget

Everything

And

Run . . . and that's my first inclination sometimes when I get uncomfortable. My favorite FEAR acronym is:

False

Evidence

Appearing

Real . . . which is what I can find in most situations if I look for the love or the lesson. I realize that most fear is from past trauma and a place within me that needs to heal. Nothing outside of love is real but we can give it power with our thoughts and actions. As discussed in this book, it's easy to fall into fear as we go through our human experience. When that happens, we can use my second favorite FEAR acronym (yes, I love acronyms):

Face

Everything

And

Rise. Any challenging situation can have a valuable love lesson attached. To rise from any situation we have to heal the past trauma and make peace on a soul level.

I also created an acronym for FIERCE to remind you how to face your fears and remember the practices in this book. How will you be FIERCE?

Fit (mentally, spiritually, and physically)?

Intentional?

Engaged?

Resourceful?

Conscious?

Empowered? Write the answers in your journal weekly and share with your family, friends, and community so they can support you in being FIERCE!

I can't promise you that bad things won't happen in your life or that fear won't ever flatten you. All I can say is that, as you are challenged and as you grow through those challenges, you will become stronger. You become a stronger person, a stronger leader, and a stronger part of the community. And you will strengthen your whole community with your inspirational growth. Don't be afraid. Not of challenges, of failure, of judgment, or of fear itself. Right here, right now, make a commitment to look fear in the face and say, "I have enough love for you. I can get through this. I know how to get through this." Do this, and you will be more than okay. You will be fierce.

ACCEPT WHO YOU ARE

1. Stand in front of a mirror, and set a timer for five minutes.

2. Look at your face in the mirror.

3. Look into your eyes and say, "I love you."

4. When the five minutes are up, write down your thoughts and feelings in your journal.

5. Do the same practice standing in front of a full-length mirror in your birthday suit. Yes, nude. Look into your eyes and admire your body while you say, "I love you."

Accepting yourself as you are, right now, will promote faster change. Accepting who I am and where I am while I'm making plans for growth is my secret weapon for lifelong evolution.

Visualize Your Best Self

What does your best self look like? Describe this here or in your journal:

_____

_____

_____

_____

Visualize a day living as your best self. What does it look like? Has it changed from earlier? Write it out.

TIME TO FLY

If you have faith that anything can happen for you, that anything can happen in your life, then it will. Don't let your fear outweigh your faith and slow your progress. Sometimes you fall. Sometimes you fly. Just promise yourself you'll never stay down. The journey will strengthen your soul. Challenges aren't meant to break you; challenges will build you if you let them. Rise, and remember you were meant to fly!

- You know fear is an opportunity for growth.
- You know your past does not define your future.
- You know how to shift from a victim mind-set to a creator mind-set.
- You know how to challenge and transform the limiting beliefs that hold you back.
- You know how to harness the power of gratitude.
- You know your soul's purpose and heart's desire.
- You know how to train your brain with affirmations.
- You know how to use visualization to manifest what it is you want.
- You know how to use faith to overcome your fears.
- You know how to use discipline to attain freedom.
- You know how to mark your successes along the way.
- You know how to use clarity and focus to accomplish your goals.
- You know how to support your total body.

You got this.

You are fierce.

The You Are Fierce Checklist

How fierce are you? See how many statements you can check off as true in your life today. Come back to this list often as you put the principles learned in this book into practice. In time you'll be checking them all!

I have

- ☐ an open mind.
- ☐ an open heart.
- ☐ a thirst for knowledge.
- ☐ a compassionate soul.
- ☐ an A-Team.

I find

- ☐ my happiness within.
- ☐ time to play.
- ☐ support through a connection to Spirit.
- ☐ the love in everything I do.
- ☐ ways to treat myself.

I am
- ☐ living a high-vibe life.
- ☐ loving as if it's the only option.
- ☐ living my Mission Statement.
- ☐ comfortable with change.
- ☐ a creator.

I do
- ☐ my best and let the chips fall where they may.
- ☐ what makes my soul sing.
- ☐ what scares me the most.
- ☐ what creates progress and forward movement.
- ☐ what supports my total body.

I feel
- ☐ my growth with each challenge.
- ☐ the vibration of love all around me.
- ☐ gratitude with each breath.
- ☐ love in every cell of my body.
- ☐ in alignment with my heart and soul.

I choose
- ☐ love over fear.
- ☐ joy over sadness.
- ☐ peace over chaos.
- ☐ creativity over competition.
- ☐ trying over failing.

My 7-Day Meal Plan

You can use this 7-Day Meal Plan as a jump start for eating a plant-based diet.

Upon Waking (on an empty stomach)

Start the day with a cleansing beverage to maximize the detox work your body performed overnight.

2 tablespoons organic key lime juice with 16 ounces water and a pinch of cayenne or 1 inch ginger, juiced (boosts immune system and aids in digestion)

OR

16 ounces celery or cucumber juice

OR

Barley grass juice extract powder with 16 ounces water

Breakfast

Greens should be consumed with every meal to naturally increase fiber intake, prevent diabetes and heart disease, and improve digestive health.

Fruit Bowl (3 to 5 fruits) with plant-based yogurt and green juice (at least 2 veggies)

OR

Gluten-free oatmeal or quinoa (1 to 4 cups) with green juice

OR

Superfood green smoothie: 16 ounces water, 1 to 2 bananas, 1 cup fruit, 1 handful greens, 1 scoop plant-based protein

OR

Heavy Metal Electric Detox Smoothie (page 180)

Snack

3 to 5 pieces of fruit (apples, oranges, bananas) with almond butter

OR

3 to 5 veggies with hummus

Lunch

1 cup protein with 3 sides of veggies (1 cup each) and 1 cup brown rice, sweet potato, quinoa, or lentils

OR

Veggie stir-fry bowl: 1/2 cup brown rice or quinoa and 3 to 5 different veggies

OR

3 to 5 different veggies, grilled

Snack

3 to 5 pieces of fruit (apples, oranges, pears)

OR

Veggies (carrots, celery, cucumber) with 1/4 cup hummus

Dinner

Big superfood salad (3 to 5 different veggies)

OR

1 cup protein with 3 sides of veggies (1 cup each)

OR

Veggie wrap (3 to 5 different veggies) with gluten-free tortilla or collard wrap or Thai-style bowl (3 to 5 different veggies)

Evening Drink

Organic elderberry tea (antiviral immune system booster)

OR

Sea moss and bladderwrack drink or capsules with green juice

Supplements

1 tablespoon spirulina per day

Vitamin B_{12}

Remember:

- Eat every 2 to 4 hours.
- Drink 3 to 4 liters of water per day.

- Eat at least 3 veggies or fruits with each meal, minimum of 5 fruits and 5 veggies per day.
- Gluten-free flour and grains only.
- Lunch is your largest meal.

EAT

All fruits

All veggies

Soy-free, gluten-free meat substitutes

High-protein starches (1 to 2 cups max per day)

Lentils	Black wild rice
Chickpeas	Sweet potatoes
Quinoa	

Fat sources (no more than 1 avocado and 2 tablespoons of oil per day)

Avocado	Coconut oil (unheated)
Nuts and seeds	Grapeseed oil (heated)
Nut butters	Olive oil (unheated)

Condiments

Balsamic vinegar	Miso (soy free)
Coconut liquid aminos	Marinara sauce
Guacamole	Salsa
Hummus	Mustard

Sweeteners

Dates	Maple syrup
Honey (local only)	Stevia (liquid form, no preservatives)

Beverages

Chai tea	Herbal tea
Coconut water	Water with lime
Green tea	

DO NOT EAT

All animal products (including meat, chicken, fish, butter, eggs, milk, and cheese)	Over 30 grams of soy per day
	Coffee more than 3 times per week (it wrecks your adrenals)
Anything with over 5 grams of saturated fat per serving	Fried food more than once a week

Chocolate more than once a week

Processed or packaged food more than once a week

Oily food (ask for oil-free everything)

All-purpose white flour

Enriched or bleached flours

Whole-wheat flour

Canola oil

Corn oil

Soybean oil

Sunflower oil

Margarine

Vegetable shortening

Ranch dressing

Mayonnaise

Ketchup

Check all food labels and avoid these ingredients. Don't forget what's on your pantry shelves now. Throw away goods that contain these:

Artificial flavors and colors

Cane sugar

Corn syrup

High-fructose corn syrup

MSG (monosodium glutamate)

Sorbitol

Xylitol

Acknowledgments

There are so many beautiful souls to whom I'm deeply grateful. I am the woman I am today because of you.

First and foremost I have to thank God, the Holy Spirit within me, and the Divine Love all around me for always supporting and guiding me when I choose love. Thank you for your unwavering compassion for me no matter how many times I get lost in the illusion of fear.

Mom and Dad, I want to acknowledge you for putting up with my unlimited amount of questions growing up. Thank you for always welcoming me home with open arms even when I went vegan and threw out all the toxic food in your house. I appreciate you because you taught me patience, compassion, and perseverance. You taught me how to never give up even when times are unbearable and I love you for that.

To my brothers and sisters, Armond, Jamar, and Talayna. We have the honor to call each other family—even when it's hard. I love you all for being you and loving me for me. Thank you for teaching me unconditional love and acceptance. I love you!

To my "Second Family," a super cool tribe of beautiful beings. You are indeed "my people" and I could not imagine doing life without you. Thank you for all the ways you show up and reflect kindness, grace, and beauty when I need them most. For your care, protection, and friendship I realize that I am blessed beyond measure: Nate Anderson, Teresa Jordan, Lonnie Jordan, Latham Thomas, Robert Reiff, Joan Van Horn, Eileen Popovich, Justin Michael Williams, Brandie Gilliam, Cameron Moore, Sanyika Calloway, Jon Morelli, Dexter Montgomery,

Rebecca Watson, Dean Ornish, Cory Booker, Troy Carter, Michael Bearden, Light Watkins, Ray Sahelian, Liana Niema, Dr. Keith Norris, Dot Todman, Jamila Underwood, Iva Stewart, Chef Ahki, Naya Rappaport, Horace Knight, Craig Cochran, Lauren Ash, and Ron Russell.

To my Hay House crew, thank you for your faith in me. Without you I could not have completed this, my first professionally published book.

To Julia, for making me a better writer by inviting me into the journey of sharing my story authentically, honestly, and fiercely. And reminding me of the gift in being an example and light to others who may have experienced the darkness that I walked through, even when I wanted to shrink back from it.

To Coleen, for always giving me honest feedback and standing in my corner to cheer me on. Thank you for your constant encouragement, advice, and support through this entire process. Your spirit is a gift to the world.

To my team, for your get-it-done attitude, stellar organizational skills, and willing hearts. I applaud and appreciate each one of you for being unicorns and always showing up for me: Njoki Maina, Emily Leikam, Camille Johnson, Marsha Micaud, and Kinsey Cathers.

I want to acknowledge, honor, and publicly appreciate every one of my mentors and inspirations. You have touched, challenged, encouraged, and changed me in so many ways and I appreciate your light in the world.

Oprah Winfrey, thank you for sharing your personal story. It proved to me that I could be great, no matter what happened to me. I am forever grateful.

Stevie Wonder, your music, consistency, and longevity in greatness inspire me daily.

India Arie, your music got me through many tough times on the journey of loving myself.

Reverend Michael Bernard Beckwith, Ricky Bernard Beckwith, and the Agape Family, thank you for being the spiritual family I needed to connect with the light within me.

Les Brown, thank you for always encouraging me to step deeper and deeper into my greatness. Your advice and encouragement sticks with me daily.

Latham Thomas, thank you for being my spiritual sister and always reminding me of my power and worth. And those 6 A.M. phone calls that inspired me to keep pushing. I am forever grateful.

Anthony William, thank you for the healing work that you do, your timely guidance, and the gift you are to the world. You are appreciated.

Michelle Obama, Iyanla Vanzant, Lisa Nicoles, Tony Robbins, Marie Forleo, Brendon Bruchard, Mairanne Williamson, Common, Steve Harvey, Alicia Keys, Dr. Sebi—the things that I once saw as insurmountable obstacles I was able to see as seeds of my growth because of your insights and advice and how you showed up in my life through the work you do. Thank you very much.

To my social media community worldwide, all I can say is WOW, and thank you for the DMs, likes, follows, and daily encouragement. You light up my life!

And, last but not least, to the women who are still yet to overcome the fears you face. My sincere prayer for you is that you will come to see that life is not conspiring against you and that all things can work for your good and growth if you would allow them to. You are stronger than your pain, more powerful than your past, and well on your way to being a fierce force in the world. I'm cheering for you and standing for you!

About the Author

Koya Webb is a conscious global citizen and heart-centered thought leader.

As a sought-after international yoga teacher, holistic health and wellness coach, motivational speaker, and professional fitness model, she is revolutionizing the holistic living landscape worldwide.

Koya believes the most important element in health is daily self-care; and only from that place can the goals of losing weight, increasing energy, and reversing life-threatening health conditions be achieved. She inspires communities worldwide to experience optimal health by practicing positive sustainable lifestyle changes each day.

Through the creation of *Get Loved Up*, a conscious community of individuals who seek to practice daily self-care and make healthy living a priority, Koya shares her passion for dramatically decreasing the number of people who suffer with chronic diseases associated with an unhealthy diet, self-defeating habits, and sedentary lifestyle through self-care, plant-based nutrition, and eco-friendly living in fun and accessible ways.

Koya is based in Beverly Hills, California, but considers the world her "home." You can connect with Koya and her conscious community at KoyaWebb.com.

We hope you enjoyed this Hay House book. If you'd like to receive our online catalog featuring additional information on Hay House books and products, or if you'd like to find out more about the Hay Foundation, please contact:

Hay House, Inc., P.O. Box 5100, Carlsbad, CA 92018-5100
(760) 431-7695 or (800) 654-5126
(760) 431-6948 (fax) or (800) 650-5115 (fax)
www.hayhouse.com® • www.hayfoundation.org

———

Published in Australia by:
Hay House Australia Pty. Ltd., 18/36 Ralph St., Alexandria NSW 2015
Phone: 612-9669-4299 • *Fax:* 612-9669-4144 • www.hayhouse.com.au

Published in the United Kingdom by:
Hay House UK, Ltd., Astley House, 33 Notting Hill Gate, London W11 3JQ
Phone: 44-20-3675-2450 • *Fax:* 44-20-3675-2451 • www.hayhouse.co.uk

Published in India by: Hay House Publishers India,
Muskaan Complex, Plot No. 3, B-2, Vasant Kunj, New Delhi 110 070
Phone: 91-11-4176-1620 • *Fax:* 91-11-4176-1630 • www.hayhouse.co.in

———

Access New Knowledge.
Anytime. Anywhere.

Learn and evolve at your own pace
with the world's leading experts.

www.hayhouseU.com

Free e-newsletters
from Hay House, the Ultimate
Resource for Inspiration

Be the first to know about Hay House's free downloads, special offers, giveaways, contests, and more!

 Get exclusive excerpts from our latest releases and videos from *Hay House Present Moments*.

 Our *Digital Products Newsletter* is the perfect way to stay up-to-date on our latest discounted eBooks, featured mobile apps, and Live Online and On Demand events.

 Learn with real benefits! *HayHouseU.com* is your source for the most innovative online courses from the world's leading personal growth experts. Be the first to know about new online courses and to receive exclusive discounts.

 Enjoy uplifting personal stories, how-to articles, and healing advice, along with videos and empowering quotes, within *Heal Your Life*.

Sign Up Now!

Get inspired, educate yourself, get a complimentary gift, and share the wisdom!

Visit www.hayhouse.com/newsletters to sign up today!